LOS ANGELES REVIEW OF BOOKS QUARTERLY JOURNAL | FALL 2014

COVER ART
SAM FALLS, UNTITLED (PAINTED PHOTOGRAMS, LATTICE 17), 2012
ACRYLIC ON ARCHIVAL PIGMENT PRINT, 24" X 20"
COURTESY OF THE ARTIST AND HANNAH HOFFMAN GALLERY

The *Los Angeles Review of Books* is a 501(c)(3) nonprofit organization. The *LARB Quarterly Journal* is published quarterly by the *Los Angeles Review of Books*, 1614 S. Central Ave., Glendale, CA 91204. Printed in Los Angeles by Janet Klein/Ace Printing. Submissions for the *Journal* can be emailed to EDITORIAL@LAREVIEWOFBOOKS.ORG. Visit our website at WWW.LAREVIEWOFBOOKS.ORG.

The *LARB Quarterly Journal* is a premium of the *LARB* Membership Program. Annual subscriptions are available. Go to WWW.LAREVIEWOFBOOKS.ORG/MEMBERSHIP for more information or email MEMBERSHIP@LAREVIEWOFBOOKS.ORG.

Distribution through Publishers Group West. If you are a retailer and would like to order the *LARB Quarterly Journal*, call 800-788-3123 or email orderentry@perseusbooks.com.

CONTENTS

< TAUBA AUERBACH, *SHADOW WEAVE– FACADE SPLIT WAVE II*, 2013
WOVEN CANVAS ON WOODEN STRETCHER, 60" x 45" (152.4 x 114.3 CM)

IAN JAMES, *UNTITLED*, 2013, PIGMENT PRINT, 13" X 19"

CATHOLIC GIRLS

JUDY CHICUREL

Today

The woman who answered the door could have been any one of our mothers. She had the kind of ashy blond hair that could have been Clairol Nice 'n Easy, or she might have had it done at a beauty parlor, like Antoine's on Main, where our own mothers went to get dolled up for weddings and holidays. Her skin was sun-washed and creased around her eyes, which made her look older than she wanted to, because she dressed young: faded straight-leg jeans rolled into cuffs above her ankles. A white Indian shirt embroidered with gold thread. Hanging silver earrings. Bare feet, with coppery polish on her toes. I tried to get a good look at her fingernails, because that's the first thing they always tell you: dirty fingernails, after you pass through the dark alley to get to the dirty table in the middle of the night. But she was holding the door halfway open and her hands were hidden.

We were standing in front of a three-story brown wood house with carved white shutters and a wraparound porch with wicker rocking chairs and a widow's watch that looked like the top tier on a wedding cake, at the high end of a road where you looked down at the ocean. Below us, the dunes rose up like small mountains and the sand really did have a silver cast, lighter and finer than the sand we were used to; that was how the town of Silverwood got its name. The houses here were farther apart than the ones in Elephant Beach, and the street was bathed in milky quiet, that special, hot summer afternoon stillness where everyone's either at the beach or huddled up inside with their air-conditioning.

"I'm — I'm here for my two o'clock appointment," Liz said. That's what Beth had told her to say. No names, no phone calls. No checks or credit cards; cash only, in an unmarked envelope.

"Come in, please," the woman said, smiling. Her voice had a lilt, like she was singing the words. She held the door open wide. Muted sunlight streamed through the windows; the gauzy curtains lifted in the breeze. In the foyer we glimpsed the living room, which had a fireplace that took up almost a whole wall, filled with egg-shaped urns of flowers. Bunches of dried starfish hung from the walls. There were window boxes on the porch as well, filled with red and purple pansies. There were candles on the mantel, on the coffee table; votives, tapers, tea lights, covered in glass and pewter.

The woman closed the door behind us, turned the lock, shot the bolt. She then opened a door on the left side of the hall and motioned us to go in. It was an office with a big desk, bookcases lining the walls, dark, slanted shades at the windows. A cushiony red love seat and chairs clustered around a small table covered with seashells of all sizes.

"Sit down, please," the woman said, sitting in the fat red chair that faced the windows. Liz sank into a corner of the love seat and I sat down next to her.

"This house, it's like spectacular, man," Liz said in some new bright voice that didn't sound like her own.

"Except for the mice in the walls," the woman said, smiling. "Who come out at night and keep us awake."

"This house is too beautiful to have mice," Liz said loudly. "This town is too beautiful to have mice running around." I turned to look at Liz. I had never heard her use this fawning, kiss-ass tone before, not to her parents or teachers or even Dr. Steadman, our high school principal, that time she was caught cutting so many classes that she almost didn't graduate.

"Maybe that's what attracts them," the woman said. "Who?" Liz asked wildly. "The mice," the woman said gently. Then she asked, "You have something for me, yes?" Liz stared at her blankly. "I said, you have something for me, yes?" the woman asked again, still smiling. I nudged Liz, tapped her purse. "Oh!" she said. "Oh! I'm so … sorry, man, really, I'm …" She rummaged in her purse and came out with an envelope. She held it out to the woman with a shaky hand. Her voice was making me sick. I wanted her to lose that fake, fawning tone and sound like Liz again.

The woman didn't take the envelope. She sat gazing at Liz. She had the calmest eyes I'd ever seen, green or gray, it was hard to tell. The light in the office was dimmer than it had been outside in the foyer, which was fine. All that streaming sunlight made me nervous. It was a perfect beach day, not a cloud in the sky. It was like a painting you could have named *July*. The breeze through the window carried the scent of the ocean. Wind chimes tinkled on the porch. The whole thing was giving me the creeps, everything so white and bright and airy. It should have been raining. The curtains should have had dirty edges, filthy hems from sweeping against a sooty windowsill. A body should have been falling out of the closet, bathed in blood. We should have come at night, in the dark, when children were asleep. But Beth had told us two o'clock on Thursday afternoon, so here we were.

The woman said, "Before we go upstairs, I'm only going to ask you once, yes? Do you want to go through with this?"

Liz took out her Marlboros, lit two, and handed me one. She began flicking ashes in the largest seashell, the kind we picked up on the beach at home all the time and used for ashtrays in our bedrooms.

"Because if you don't, you can walk back out that door right now and that's the end of it," the woman said. She didn't sound mad. She didn't look like she cared one way or the other.

Liz blew smoke up at the ceiling fan. Beneath the huge frames of her sunglasses, her cheeks were still stained and splotchy from crying on the bus.

"I can tell you this is safer and less painful than childbirth, and will take far less time than a root canal," the woman said. I could see the corners of Liz's mouth turn down, her lips begin to tremble.

The woman focused on me. "And you are her good friend, yes?" I nodded.

"And no matter what goes down in the next few minutes, you both know that whatever happens here is confidential, not to be talked about outside of this house, or I could lose my medical license and that's one less option for women to be safe."

The word "safe" echoed through the cool room. I thought it was a strange choice of words. It was not a word I would have chosen. It was only after she'd spoken those words that I realized the woman was the doctor. I had thought she was a nurse, an assistant, someone who took care of the preliminaries. I thought the doctor would be short and mannish-looking, with pinched lips and close-cropped dark hair and lines in her forehead, wearing a dirty white coat. I wondered if the woman had children herself, if she sent them to day camp or to the beach with a babysitter, with strict instructions not to come home before a certain time. Or if they were grown, our age, and suspected but weren't sure what was going on in their own house. I tried to imagine how I would feel if I suddenly found out my mother was performing abortions in the basement or out in the backyard shed. I couldn't imagine it. I couldn't get my mind around such a thing. There were no family pictures on the doctor's desk, in the office room. There were no pictures of real people anywhere around.

The woman put her elbows on her knees, rested her chin in her hands. Liz crushed her cigarette in the shell on the coffee table. A single spark refused to die. She took a deep breath.

"Okay, man," she said. "Let's do it. Let's do it now." She sounded like Liz again. She stood up and held the envelope out again. This time the woman took it. She went to the desk, opened a drawer, and the envelope disappeared. She walked to the door and opened it, then beckoned us through with a graceful finger. I'd been so engrossed in looking around that until now I'd forgotten to look at her hands. She wasn't wearing polish on her fingernails. They were cut short and square. They looked short and square and strong and clean.

Last Monday

"You swear on your mother's life you didn't tell Beth it was me?" Liz asked Nanny for like the 90th time.

We were sitting in the Shot Glass Saloon up in the Point, at the other end of Elephant Beach. It was dark and dim and everyone looked familiar even though we didn't know them. We'd purposely come here because it was several miles from the Trunk and anyone we would run into. Even so, Liz had insisted on us wearing dark sunglasses and black jeans and T-shirts and bandannas so that no one would recognize us. It was 4:30 in the afternoon and we were sitting at a table in the corner, drinking whiskey sours on the rocks and planning Liz's abortion. She'd gotten pregnant after balling Cory in an AMC Gremlin, her least favorite car on her father's lot, but the only one that had been available. It had been a cramped and hurried encounter; she said she wished it had happened in the Pontiac Bonneville, classically restored and big and roomy as a bed, but it was a premium seller and Cory was afraid her father might notice something was amiss. When she'd told Cory she was late, he'd just nodded and said, "Bummer." The next day he gave her 200 dollars and told her, "More where that came from if you need it, just get it taken care of. I don't want to know the details."

Nanny shook her head. "I told you," she said patiently. "Beth doesn't want to know. She says the less people know, the better. She'll make the call and set up the appointment. Then she'll get back to me with the day and time."

"How does Beth know her again?" I asked. Beth Fagan was in her last year of nursing school at Joshua Stern Medical Center in Manhattan; she'd been the midwife at Maggie Mayhew's home birth. She said it was a deep and life-changing experience, even though everything had gone wrong and Aunt Francie said it was a miracle the baby had been born at all.

"From Joshua Stern," Nanny said. "It's kind of like an underground thing, but all the nurses know about it."

"If it's so underground, what's she doing living in Silverwood?" Liz asked.

Nanny snorted. "Would you think to go looking for an abortion doctor in Silverwood?"

"So, what, I just knock on the door and say, 'Hey man, I'm, like, here for my abortion'?"

"Pretty much, yeah. Beth will tell us everything we need to do."

"And she doesn't have to know my name or anything?" Liz squinted through the cigarette smoke.

"She doesn't want to know your name," Nanny whispered. "Because if anything happens, she could lose her license, go to jail —"

Liz was staring hard at Nanny. "What is this 'if anything happens'? What's going to happen? If nobody's looking in Silverwood for this abortion doctor, then please, somebody tell me, what the fuck is going to happen?"

"Lower your voice," Nanny hissed. Heads at the bar were beginning to lift and look us over.

Sure enough, the cocktail waitress came by. Her face had that creased look of too many cigarettes and her voice was chipped and hoarse. "Everything all right over here?" she asked, and Liz burst into tears. Nanny and I looked at each other helplessly. The waitress peeled off some cocktail napkins from the stack on her tray and handed them to Liz. The napkins had "The Shot Glass Saloon" written in bold red script, and beneath the letters, a cowboy brandishing a six-shooter, standing next to an old-timey saloon with swinging doors. There were no cowboys in the Shot Glass, only drunks with nothing better to do than sit at the bar drinking boilermakers, listening to Frank Sinatra's voice from the jukebox singing "It Was a Very Good Year" 47 times.

The waitress looked at me and Nanny. "Boyfriend problems?" she asked. She lit a cigarette and laid it on her tray with the smoking end outward.

Nanny looked at me. "Kind of," I told her. The minute she'd missed her period, Liz had started planning her wedding. The ceremony would be on Comanche Beach at sunset, and the reception would take place at the new Knights of Columbus catering hall, right on the bay. Liz would wear a red velvet granny dress with a matching crown of roses in her hair. We'd all be bridesmaids and wear any shade of velvet we wanted, except green, so it didn't look like Christmas. Cory would get promoted to manager of her father's dealership and they'd buy the house that had been for sale forever on Weber Avenue, by the bay, where all the bedrooms faced the water. Even though Cory McGill had never taken Liz to dinner, met her mother, or hung out with any of her friends.

The waitress looked at Liz and nodded. Her eyes were winged with eyeliner at the corners and her roots were showing through at the crown, at her temples. She dragged heavily on her cigarette, placed it back on the rim of her cocktail tray, laid the tray down, and put her hands on our table.

"Let me tell you girls something about men," she said. "They're all a hundred years out of the trees, and there's not a goddamned thing you can do about it."

Last Night

The night before, Liz and Nanny were supposed to come to my house so we could go over our plans for the hundredth time. We were going to take the bus; Liz didn't want to drive in case anyone recognized her car, even though Silverwood was at the other end of Long Island and no one we knew ever hung out there. After it was over, we'd be staying overnight at the Dancing Dolphin Motel; Nanny had the good idea to call the Chamber of Commerce and get a recommendation. It sounded funky and cheerful, and we told our parents we were taking the train to the city to shop at Macy's and see a movie, maybe *The Godfather*, and stay overnight at Nanny's grandmother's apartment in Washington Heights. Liz still insisted on us wearing our incognito outfits, even though I tried telling her we'd only draw attention to ourselves since nobody in Elephant Beach wore black in summer unless they were going to a funeral. Liz thought that if we wore our black bandannas and shades either no one would recognize us or they'd think we were too crazy to deal with and leave us alone.

We usually didn't hang out at my house, because I lived farther away from Comanche Beach and Eddy's and all our other hangouts. But Liz didn't want to talk at her house, and Nanny was terrified of her mother overhearing us, since the walls of their bungalow were thin. Wednesday was my mother's mah-jongg night so she and her friends would be playing in the kitchen and wouldn't have heard a bomb go off once they got going. We would have the back porch to ourselves. I waited out there, lying on the chaise lounge, munching on mah-jongg food, nonpareils, and M&M's, reading a book about growing up in the 1950s when life was simpler with happier endings.

"What, no street corner tonight?" My mother came out on the back porch, shaking the dry mop over the porch railing.

"Nope," I said, chomping on a nonpareil. I felt safe, knowing she wouldn't start in on me with her friends due to arrive any minute. "Liz is coming over, we're gonna just hang out, take it easy."

"Let me have a cigarette," she said, leaning against the railing. On my 18th birthday she had given me permission to smoke because she was tired of me stinking up the bathroom with hair spray to hide the smell; that drove my father crazy. She didn't smoke much herself, only when she played mah-jongg or canasta. But sometimes, when I came home late and she was sitting in the kitchen doing the crossword puzzle, we'd have a cigarette together and talk about things. Her voice always sounded younger then, especially when she put her hands over her mouth so that the sound of her laughter wouldn't wake my brother or my father.

My mother lit the cigarette and inhaled deeply, leaning against the porch railing, gazing up at the sky. I lit one, too, to be sociable, even though I'd just had one.

"What's with Liz lately?" she asked me. "She sounded upset when she called before. What is she, having boyfriend trouble?"

I sighed. "Kind of," I said.

"The trouble with you girls is, you make everything too easy for these boys," she said. "Make them work a little, then they won't treat you like a pair of old shoes."

"Mom —"

"I know, I know, the mothers, we never know anything," she said. "You wonder why I get so upset with you running down to that corner every night. I want you to expect more out of life, not less. But who knows," she said, the smoke from her cigarette curling above her head like a gauzy crown, "maybe it's our fault as much as yours. If we had more to give you, you'd expect more. You do the best you can, but sometimes it's not enough."

I looked at my mother, surprised. She always talked like we were better than other people we knew, certainly than the people I hung out with. But there were things we didn't have; my father refused to buy anything on credit because he'd grown up poor and seen too many repossessions. Our television was black-and-white, and we had a washing machine, but not a dryer. I liked hanging my jeans over the porch railing and letting them dry there; they always smelled like the sun. Billy once told me that I had the best-smelling clothes of any girl he knew. But if I told that to my mother, she'd only ask me why Billy knew that in the first place, and how close was he getting to my clothes anyway, that he could smell them so good.

"Where are you?" my mother asked. She sounded annoyed. "Have you even heard one word I've said?"

"I was just thinking how I like the way my jeans smell from hanging on the porch in the sun," I told her.

"What on earth made you think of that?" she asked.

"Only that if we had a clothes dryer they wouldn't smell as good," I said. "I'd kind of miss it."

My mother looked at me for a long moment. Then she smiled. "Next you'll want me to hunt up Grandma's old washboard and do the washing out here instead of throwing the clothes in the machine," she said, laughing. She came over and hugged me close, something she rarely did anymore. I hugged her back, and felt tears pushing up against my eyelids.

"You're such a good girl, such a good kid," she whispered against my hair. "I only want the best for you, can you see that? You think all I do is carp and criticize, but I only want the best."

"I know," I whispered back. My mother held me for a moment longer, then kissed the side of my head and pushed herself away. "Go back to your book," she said, and went into the house, closing the screen door softly behind her.

About 20 minutes later, I heard the doorbell over the sound of my mother and her friends chattering. Then Liz came banging through the screen door, her mouth stuffed with Almond Joy miniatures. The air was filled with the sound of cicadas and the voices of some kids playing stickball in the street.

Liz said, around a mouthful of chocolate, "Man, you know I love your mother, but why does she always sound, like, angry?"

"You're just feeling sensitive," I said, but I knew it was true. My mother was the youngest of four kids. My grandparents hadn't wanted her; they were poor and lived in one of those old-timey tenements on the Lower East Side and my grandfather worked three jobs and was going to night school to learn English when he could fit it in. In those days, they believed that a bumpy trolley-car ride would bring on a miscarriage; my grandmother rode the trolley as much as she could afford to, but it didn't work. For her first year, my mother slept in the bottom drawer of my grandparents' dresser as there was no room or money for more beds. Maybe the reason she yelled at us so much was because, despite the odds, she'd managed to make her way into the world, and she wanted everyone to know she was here to stay.

"Where's Nanny?" I asked Liz.

Liz sat down in the beach chair opposite me. "Nanny bailed because she thinks I'm going to hell and she will, too, if she comes along for the ride."

"Oh, she did not —"

"Yeah, she did." Liz sighed. "She said there's some christening she has to go to tomorrow, her mother's dragging them all into the city."

I wondered about this. I'd thought it odd that Nanny hadn't returned my call from yesterday, because we usually spoke daily and now there was all this going on. I guessed she was thinking she'd see me tonight and we'd talk then.

"Well, you know how it is with family stuff, and Mrs. Devlin —"

"Katie." Liz shook her head like I was an idiot. "Tomorrow's Thursday. You ever hear of a christening taking place on a Thursday? You ever hear of a christening that gave everyone, like, one day's notice?"

The night smelled heavily of honeysuckle. Liz got up and walked over to the porch railing. She stood there, gazing down at my mother's tomato plants. She was quiet for a long time. Finally, she said, "I think — I think there's something wrong with me, man. I mean, really, I —" She broke off, looked up at the darkening sky. "I mean, when I found out, when I knew for sure? Before I told anyone? I was, like, so happy. I — I really thought, right, I really thought that we'd have a wedding on the beach, that he'd be the manager of my father's dealership. That I'd be buying hanging crystals from Heads Up for the baby's room, all that shit." She shook her head. "We call you the space shot, you live in your head so much, but I'm the one living on cloud fucking nine."

The light of day was dying, slowly, leaving inky smudges in the sky. I wanted to walk over and put my arms around her, but Liz never liked being touched; she shrugged off embraces, even on her birthday, was the first to scream, "Lezzie!" if you even laid a hand on her arm. I leaned back and lit a cigarette.

"I thought maybe if I told my mother," Liz said. I sat up and stared at her. Mrs. McGann was the same age as the rest of our parents but she seemed older. Her hair was iron gray and she never visited Antoine's on Main because, she said, if God had meant for your hair to stay the same color all your life, he would have made it so. Mr. and Mrs. McGann went to Mass every morning, not just on Sundays. They believed in everything the Church said. They believed that the Holy Communion wafer was the body of Jesus. I saw Mrs. McGann's face one Sunday as she walked back from taking Communion up on the altar. I had never seen her smile that way before. She looked — transported. She looked like she was in a much better world than the one the rest of us lived in.

"I thought maybe if I told my mother," Liz said, "she'd see it my way, you know, help me have the baby. I mean, let's face it, she'd much rather I had the baby than — than this." She blew ragged smoke rings out over the garden. "And then I thought, what am I, nuts? She'd rather I was dead. She'd rather I was dead than having a baby with no husband, than — than any of it."

"Liz," I said.

"Don't 'Liz' me, you know it's true." Liz leaned forward on the railing, away from me. I couldn't see her face. "She'd ship me off someplace for sure, some home for unwed mothers in fucking Nebraska or someplace, as far away as possible, make me put it up for adoption, then make me come home and go to church with her every morning and wear a big scarlet 'A' for asshole every day around the house. I'd never hear the end of it." She lit another cigarette, and, even from where I was sitting, I could see her hands shaking. She threw the match into the air so that it would land below us, in the tomatoes and lettuce and green peppers.

Every night before dinner, I would go down to the garden and pick vegetables for the salad. I liked the smell of things growing in the earth.

"That's what would happen, all right," Liz was saying, her voice bitter. "My parents would love Jesus no matter what he did, but they would never love me again. They send money to save the innocent babies in the Congo, but they would never love their unmarried daughter's baby." She shook her head back and forth. I didn't say anything. I knew Liz's parents. I knew what she said was true. "I can just see my mother's face. My father — hey, he hardly knows I'm around now, right? I mean, if I told him? Like, tried to force Cory into a — a shotgun situation, some shit like that?" She snorted. "My father would blame me. I bet you my next paycheck that's what would happen. And Cory, it's like he wasn't even worried about that. Wasn't even worried that I might tell my father, that he would — because he knows, right? He sees it every day, the way my father treats me. You've seen him, the way he acts. And once this happened, it's like I wouldn't even exist. And my mother, that look on her face —"

"Liz," I said. "Liz, come on, man. You didn't do anything wrong, okay? You loved someone, you didn't do anything wrong."

"Says the virgin," she said, sighing. She came over and sat down next to me on the chaise. We sat like that for a while, listening to my mother's friends laughing, the clink of coffee cups, forks scraping the last little bits of Sara Lee chocolate layer cake from their plates. Liz's head was bent so far down it was almost touching the floor. I had to lean forward to hear what she was saying.

"I need to know you're with me, Katie," she said. "I mean, I thought you were going to be the one to bag out in the first place."

"Liz —"

"I've heard you say it! 'If abortion was around, I wouldn't be here today.' I've heard you say it a hundred times."

"I never said it a hundred —"

"Katie, I know you," she whispered fiercely. "You're so fucking dramatic —"

"I'm so fucking dramatic?" I said, thinking of the crown of roses, the red velvet wedding dress.

"In your head, you're more dramatic than the rest of us," she whispered. "What happens when we get there? What if you're sitting around waiting and you start thinking it's you I'm killing and not —"

"Stop it!" I whispered, just as fierce. "Shut the fuck up right now or I'll —"

"I need to know," she said savagely. "I need to know if you're with me, because if you're not, it's cool, no, really, man, it is; I can do this by myself, but you have to tell me now. I don't want to feel all safe when I go to sleep tonight and then find out that I'm —" Her head dropped lower, her hair spilling over the porch floor. I lit another cigarette. Wherever my mother was now, the one who'd given me up so I could have a better life, she hadn't been in the smokers' bathroom at school that day when Barbara Malone began yanking the hair from my scalp like a deranged warrior, or jumped on Barbara's back, threatening to dunk her head in a toilet bowl if she didn't leave me alone. But Liz had. It was Liz who lit my first cigarette, brought me down to Comanche Street, gave me a place to belong. I started to say something, but stopped when I saw her face. It was contorted, her lips quivering, her eyes dry but darting wildly, as if seeking shelter. I took hold of her hands, held them hard against my heart.

"I'm here, man," I said. "I'm here, I swear. I swear on my mother's life."

Liz nodded, then gently removed her hands from mine. After a while she whispered, "To think I wanted him to marry me." She covered her face with her hands, and the sound of her sobbing was drowned out by the crashing of tiles against the kitchen table, the triumphant cry of "Mah-jongg!" by one of my mother's friends.

The Next Morning

Liz insisted we take the 7:27 bus; the few of our friends' parents who worked in the city, including my father, took the 7:55 train that left from the same station, so we'd miss having to run into any of them. No one else we knew got up that early except the surfers and they'd be in the ocean, not at the bus station. She wanted to check into the motel and get her bearings before heading over to the doctor's place. We had the address but no phone number; the doctor refused to speak to her clients on the phone. "We can pretend it's like a vacation," Liz said. I agreed, even though it wasn't like we were going to Aruba or someplace. Silverwood was only about two hours away, one of the arty beach towns where painters and writers supposedly had summer places.

There was a thin streamer of gold against the sky as we walked out to the buses after buying our tickets. I paused for a minute to look at the sky, thinking, when you lived by the water, even the bus station could look beautiful in the early morning light.

"Well, well, look who's here," I heard, and turned to see Mitch, leaning on a trash dumpster while he tried to light a cigarette. He was wearing his military-issue sunglasses.

"What the fuck is he doing here?" Liz whispered, panicked. "I thought he never left Comanche Street."

"What are you doing here?" I asked Mitch. My voice sounded loud in my own ears.

He exhaled and began hobbling over to where we were standing. Away from Comanche Street, he looked taller, straighter, his cane making him seem more distinguished, even though the closer he got, you could smell the booze and sweat.

"Had a rough night," he said, his voice sounding like crunched gravel. "Couldn't get to sleep even after the bar closed; fucking birds were on the ledge outside, sounded like they were in the room, for chrissake. I'm due for a visit to the VA hospital to stock my meds and make sure I'm still alive, so instead of killing a whole damn day I'll only kill a whole damn morning, can you dig it? At least the goddamned train is air-conditioned. But the real question is, where are you two fine beauties off to at this time of the morning? And what's with the funereal garb?"

Liz mumbled, "Later, man," and began walking to the opposite end of the station, where the buses were parked.

"I better get going," I said. "So we don't miss the bus."

I could feel Mitch's eyes watching me behind his sunglasses. He scratched the stubble on his chin. Finally, he asked, "There something you want to tell me, baby doll?"

"Like what?" I asked innocently.

"I don't know," he said. "That's why I asked. Everything all right with you and Sister Morphine over there?" He jerked his head in Liz's direction. "Not like her to be so quiet."

"No, we're cool," I said. "She's just not into being up this early. Thing is, we both have to be to work in the afternoon and we have to buy a — a birthday present for one of our friends from school, you wouldn't know her, they're having a surprise party for her next weekend and this was the only time —"

"Shine it on, darlin'," he said softly. "I get the drift."

I felt my insides relax a little. "Listen, don't tell anyone you saw us, okay?"

Mitch nodded, watching me from behind his sunglasses.

"All right, later," I said, but he pulled me back as I turned to go. He fumbled in his pocket and came up with a 20-dollar bill and held it out. "Here," he said. "Buy yourselves some lunch or something."

"C'mon, man, I don't want your money," I said, but he shoved the bill into my hand, crumpling it between my fingers. "Take it," he said, his voice low and steely.

You live over a bar, I wanted to say. *You sleep on torn sheets. You wake up screaming in the night.* "Thanks," I whispered instead. I could feel my throat begin to tremble. I kissed his cheek quickly and then turned and began walking toward Liz and the bus that would take us to Silverwood.

Liz hadn't said much on the way to the bus station and she wasn't saying much as we rolled onto the Meadowbrook Parkway. She just kept lighting cigarettes, staring out the window. The bus wasn't very crowded; most of the seats were empty but we were still sitting way in the back. It's funny, but the people I hang out with, we always gravitate to the back of everything: classrooms, movie theaters, buses. There was a young mother with four kids sitting near the middle, all redheads, and two of them looked like twins. They were keeping her pretty busy, climbing all over the seats, clamoring for juice and cookies, hitting each other. But outside of that, it was pretty quiet.

I thought about my own mother, the one who gave me up. I always pictured her brushing her long, black hair, staring out the window, waiting for someone. Sometimes, I pictured her sitting at a scarred brown vanity table, staring into the scratched mirror, dressed only in a bra and girdle with her flesh bulging between the elastic borders, a glass of something amber by her side. She looked sad like that, staring into the mirror. Had she thought about doing something like this? Had she gone for a two-hour bus ride alone or with her best friend and then chickened out halfway there? Or stood in an alley outside the doctor's door and then fled before even knocking? Or made it as far as the table and then gotten so hysterical that the stern-faced, short-haired, thin-lipped doctor had thrown up her hands and said, "I can't do this, here, take your money and go"? I never thought about my father, except when people told me I looked part Indian, especially in the summer when I tanned very dark. I thought maybe he'd been part of the Shinnecock tribe we'd studied in Local History at school. My mother had been a good Catholic girl. I'd been adopted through St. Joseph's Sanctuary in Fog River, a home for unwed mothers behind a huge brick wall not far from the ferry. I thought about what would have happened if she'd kept me. Would she stand in the doorway of the bathroom while I put on my mascara, screaming that I'd end up living over a bar with six kids if I kept hanging around street corners? Sometimes lately when I looked in the mirror I wondered if she'd recognize me walking down the street, if there was enough of her in me for that to happen. But when I thought about her, it wasn't a burning in my heart, the way it was when I thought about Luke. I wouldn't be thinking about her now if I wasn't on my way to an abortion doctor.

I was so into my thoughts I didn't realize at first that my seat was rocking. I thought something had broken loose and the seat needed adjusting. Then I realized it was Liz. She was shaking so bad that the seats were vibrating.

"Jesus, Liz," I said. I thought maybe she had a fever and we would have to call the whole thing off. I put my hand on her arm, and she grabbed hold of me.

"Nanny's right, I'm going to hell," she said, speaking fast, in a low voice. "After this, it's the only place for me. I'm going to hell and there's nothing, not one goddamned thing I can do to save myself."

"Liz —"

"I know I did a lot of bad things in my life, but I always thought I could make it up later, you know, when we got older. But I can never make this up. I can never save my soul after this. Best thing that could happen, I die on the table, right in the middle —"

"Stop it!" I said, grabbing her shoulders. "Stop it right now! You're not going to die, it's a clean, safe place —"

"Yeah, yeah, so clean, you could eat off it, like my mother says," she said bitterly. "Maybe we could have a dinner party after I — WILL YOU SHUT THAT FUCKING KID UP!" she screamed suddenly, jumping out of her seat. "SHUT HIM UP! SHUT HIM UP, GODDAMNIT!"

One of the red-haired kids had been crying, but now he stopped mid-wail, abruptly and completely. Everyone was looking at us, including the driver in his rearview mirror. Liz sat down, lit another cigarette, and went back to staring out the window. She had stopped shaking.

The mother of the crying kid was coming at us, snorting fire. I ran up the aisle before she could reach Liz, blocking her way.

"Out of my way," she said, eyes blazing. "Just who the hell does she think she is, yelling about my kid like that?"

"Look, I'm sorry," I said, talking fast, "she's upset. She's upset and —"

"Huh!" the mother said. "She don't look too upset to me. She —" "She's — we're on our way to a funeral," I said. "It's — it's someone close to her, very close, and she's just — she's really not herself." Now I was glad we were dressed in black so the funeral story would be more believable.

"I don't care what she is," the mother said. "She's got no right —"

"Her nephew," I whispered. "It's her favorite nephew. She can't stand even being around — I mean, your kids, they remind her —"

The mother stared at Liz, her eyes narrowed.

"Since it happened, she's been like — she has these outbursts ..." I trailed off and raised my eyebrows, trying to make it sound like Liz was one step away from the county asylum.

"How old was the nephew?" the mother whispered.

"Four," I said. "Only four years old. It was so tragic, it was —"

"My God, how did it happen?" the mother whispered. But my imagination was suddenly exhausted. "I can't talk about it," I said, making my voice sound sorrowful. "I'm sorry, but it's just too — I just can't —"

"Sure, sure, I understand," she said, patting my shoulder. "Well. We all have our days. Had a few myself. You can imagine, with this crowd." She jerked her head toward the kids, who were watching her, open-mouthed. "Tell your friend I'm sorry for her loss." She turned and walked toward her children. She took the two smallest ones with the reddest hair on her lap and began talking softly to them. They were all quiet, listening, their eyes wandering back toward Liz, who was staring out the window.

I walked to my seat and sat down. I put my arm around Liz's shoulders. For once, she didn't flinch. She leaned against me and closed her eyes. We rode like that the rest of the way.

Right Now

The room was hidden from the rest of the house. It was the widow's watch at the top, connected to a small staircase behind an oak closet in the bathroom, so small that it seemed made for children, not adults. "I feel like Anne fucking Frank," Liz muttered as we climbed into the space. I smiled. I was happy that Liz sounded like Liz again.

Prisms of light danced from the tiny triangular windows. Bottles of colored glass hung from the walls, casting violet shadows against wide, weathered planks that looked like whitewashed driftwood. In the center of the room was a narrow bed dressed in white. And above the bed, something we hadn't been able to see from the street: a skylight.

There was a portable metal table against one wall, covered with a white cloth, and on the shelf above the table, a tape player; strains of Joni Mitchell singing "California" floated through the air. A woman younger than the doctor was standing by the table, assembling instruments, checking things over. She wore jeans, a white peasant top, and flip-flops.

The doctor gestured toward her and said, "My assistant," and I remembered: no names. When the woman turned toward us and smiled, my heart sank; she looked almost exactly like Marily Weiss, a girl at Elephant Beach High School who Liz hated with a passion because she had told Mrs. Jacovides, the home ec teacher, that Liz was trying to copy her answers on a quiz when Liz really wasn't. One time, Marily came into the smoking bathroom by mistake — you could tell by looking at her that she'd never smoked a cigarette in her life — and Liz threatened to wrap her tongue around her tonsils for telling lies and started coming toward her, and Marily screamed and ran out of the bathroom without even taking a piss. I was hoping Liz wouldn't notice the resemblance, but now she was lying on the bed while the doctor swabbed her arm with cotton, holding a needle in her hand. "Valium," she explained. "Within five minutes or so it should be taking effect." Liz was lying very still beneath the white sheet, staring with great interest at the skylight in the ceiling.

The doctor and her assistant slipped white coats on over their clothes, which made me feel better. It was still too quiet.

"Was that skylight always here?" I asked, staring at the slippery light pouring down. The doctor turned toward me and smiled. "No, I had that put in when I bought the house. It was much too dark in here because these windows are so small. I wanted natural light."

I looked around at the colored bottles and the driftwood walls and suddenly I was wildly angry. I wanted to smash all the instruments on the metal table, smack the doctor hard and jolt that serene look out of her face, the calmness out of her eyes. It was great to talk about light and keeping women safe, but just because you covered it all up with candles and wind chimes and skylights didn't mean nothing bad would ever happen. It didn't mean that people wouldn't get hurt or die. I heard a vague sound, like scratching in the walls, and I thought of the mice, mewling, hungry, waiting for everyone to go to bed so they could start scavenging. But maybe it wasn't mice after all. Maybe it was the sound of the babies, little ghost babies huddled together for warmth, having no idea where they were. Frightened, crying for their mothers.

"Are you all right?" the doctor asked me, looking concerned.

"Just Jim-fucking-dandy," I said. She looked at me for a long moment. Behind us, the assistant folded Liz's clothes carefully and placed them on a shelf. I wondered if Liz noticed her resemblance to Marily Weiss and if she was too stoned to think about punching her in the face.

The doctor sighed, rolling up her sleeves, busying herself with the tray. "Women," she said, shaking her head. "They'd rather you wrap it all up in dirty sheets and ribbons of blood. And we wonder why men treat us like dirt." She spoke softly, her lips barely moving. But I heard every word. I started to speak, but then I heard Liz's voice.

"Katie, where are you? Are you still here?" Her voice sounded loose, dreamy. The doctor and I walked toward the bed from opposite directions.

"You're staying with me, right, Katie?" Liz turned her eyes on the doctor. "She can stay, can't she?"

"Do you want to stay here with your friend or wait downstairs?" the doctor asked me. "There's a small room, right across from the bathroom, with books, magazines. One of us will come and get you when we're done here."

"She's staying," Liz said, closing her eyes. "Katie, man, tell her you're staying here in the room with me. I love this room. I could live in this room. Katie, are you still here? Where are you?" I didn't want to stay. I wanted to go home. I didn't want to be in this room one more minute, but all day Liz had been slipping in and out of herself and I was afraid she might disappear completely if I left her.

"I'm here," I said, so loudly the assistant looked up. She had almost the exact same snotty look on her face that Marily Weiss did most of the time. I hoped Liz wouldn't open her eyes in the middle and see that look.

"I'm here. What should I do?" I asked the doctor, feeling panicky. There weren't any chairs in the room. I didn't want to just stand there, watching. I wanted to close my eyes and when I opened them again, I wanted it to be over.

"You can stand behind her and massage her shoulders," the doctor said briskly, moving down the length of the bed. "Help her relax, though she seems to be doing fine with the Valium. Yes, just like that. Just like that."

I stood behind Liz, kneading her shoulders. Her flesh felt soft and light beneath my hands. In the background, Mick Jagger was singing "Wild Horses." The first time I'd heard the song was at Liz's house, in her bedroom, after we'd smoked a joint and she put the headphones over my ears and said, "Just listen, man, it's like — like listening to a waterfall tripping over tiny stones in a stream." I closed my eyes and started humming along to the music.

After

And then it was over almost before it began. I thought the whole thing would take hours. I thought everything would take hours; when I pictured Luke and me in his bed making love, his honey-colored skin covering mine, it started out with golden light at the windows and ended with sunset colors crowding the sky. But then I remembered Liz telling us about her brief, passionate couplings with Cory McGill and how Nanny said her first time with Voodoo lasted as long as it took to drink an ice cream soda. How long does it take to drink an ice cream soda, even if you drag it out with a few cigarettes in between? A new thought occurred to me, that women had all this drama, all this waiting and hoping and crying over things we'd been told, raised on, warned about, these monumental milestones that ended up lasting only minutes in our lives and were never, ever as wonderful or horrible as you thought they would be.

"Beautiful," the doctor was saying. I thought that, once again, she'd chosen a word that seemed out of place. I opened my eyes but I didn't see anything. I listened for a minute, but there was no sound coming from the walls. The doctor was patting Liz's leg.

"Everything is fine," she said. "I want you to rest a bit, then I'll do a final check and you're all done." She left the room, closing the door behind her. The assistant snapped the sheet off the bed and placed a brighter one over Liz. I saw the bloodstains on the old sheet, like fresh tracks in the snow, before the assistant bunched it up and threw it in a blue wicker hamper in the corner.

For the first time since we came into the room, I looked directly into Liz's face. She looked pale and tired, but her eyes were clear. Later, at the motel, she'd tell me how at one point she'd felt the room grow dark and thought it was raining. She could hear the rain beating down hard on the bed, soaking her skin, her clothes, even though she felt dry. The raindrops sounded like individual bullets, and in her mind she saw herself facing a firing squad in front of Eddy's candy store on Comanche Street. They kept shooting at her from across the street. Even though they were strangers, she could see by their faces they were frustrated because she wouldn't go all the way down. They finally turned around and began walking away. Liz said she could feel herself smiling, proud that she had fooled them. She felt a twinge of pain, but it was only a nick where a bullet had grazed her thigh without breaking the skin. There wouldn't even be a scar.

Up above, the sky seemed gray and overcast, as though it might really rain. We watched the gulls circling the roof, heard their beggarly cries through the tiny windows. I was careful not to touch Liz. I was afraid if I touched her something might break.

"How you doing, man?" I whispered.

She leaned forward and whispered something back. I leaned closer and said, "Louder."

Liz put her lips hard against my ear. "Who invited Marily Weiss's twin fucking sister? Should I wrap her tongue around her tonsils?" We started laughing. We laughed until we became hysterical, leaning into each other, snorting, gasping, until tears poured down our cheeks. The doctor came into the room, smiling. She said to Liz, "This will only take a minute." She stood at the foot of the bed, waiting, and even when she stopped smiling, when she finally said in a sharper voice than we'd heard her use all day, "All right, girls, that's enough," still we couldn't stop laughing, as the rain finally began to fall and we heard it beating against the light from the sky.

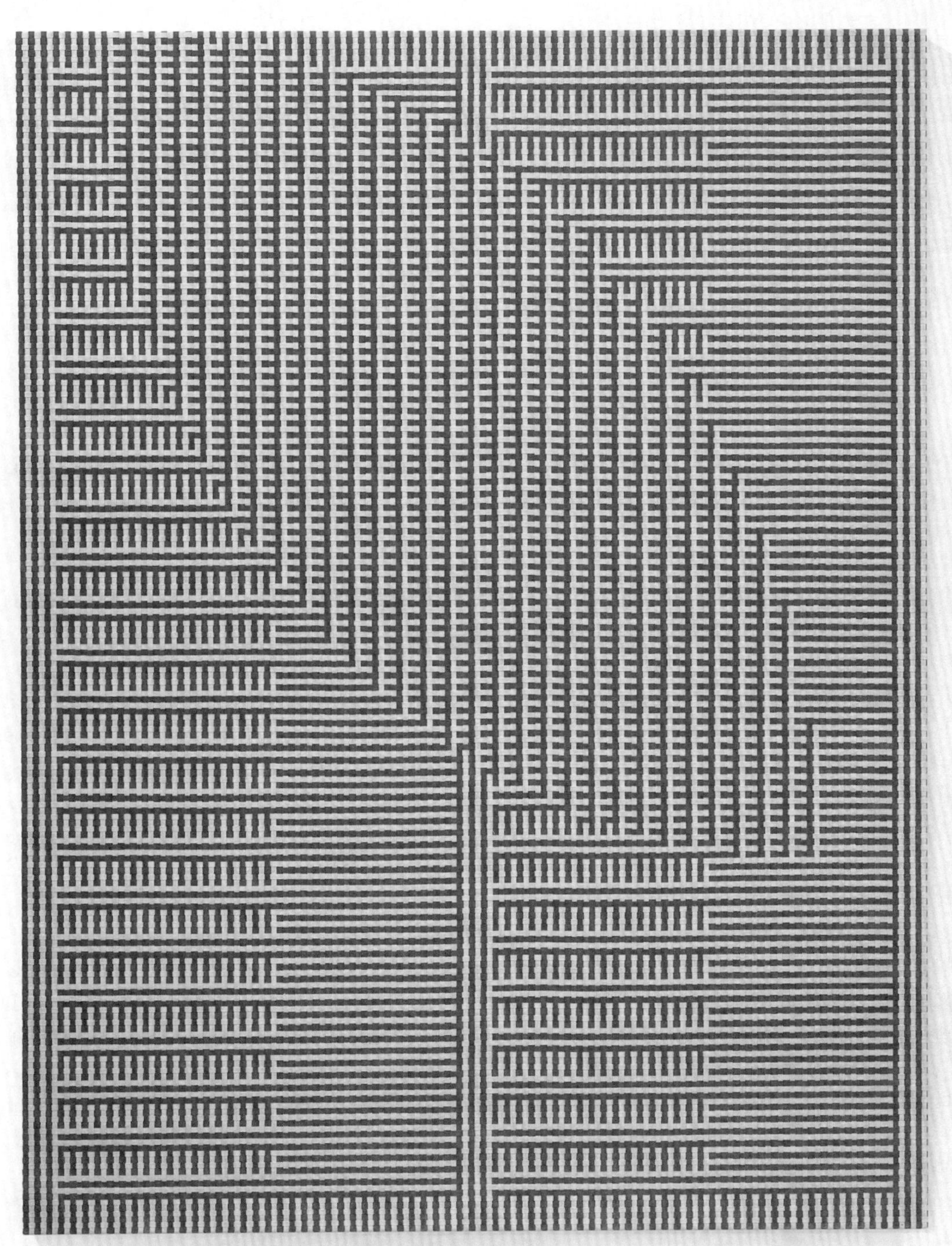

TAUBA AUERBACH, *SHADOW WEAVE—HOLE, GHOST I*, 2013
WOVEN CANVAS ON WOODEN STRETCHER, 60" X 45" (152.4 x 114.3 CM)

BETH'S UNCLE

AIMEE BENDER

Beth's uncle was handsome, and young, and it was weird that he was her uncle, given that he was maybe only seven years older than we were. He fit the movie genre older brother/cousin type, handing out cigarettes in her basement, sneaking booze into paper cups from a silver flask. He maybe had seen too many of those movies himself, because he did it up to exact likeness. And we had seen the movies too, so we all fell for him, but I think we would've without the movies. I would've. I would lie in bed at night and think about his nose, the slope of his nose, and how it ended bluntly at the tip in a way I found both endearing and exciting and it was about all this young girl could handle then in terms of appreciation of a bodily protrusion belonging to a male.

What happened wasn't bad, but it was ordinariness to the point that it became squalid or just depressing: he failed out of the neighboring community college and came to work at the local hardware store and then was caught for stealing from the register and went to prison for six months and then married a woman who called him a rug rat and his handsomeness dissolved under french fries and too much sun and only that tip of the nose remained. Still, by that point, I had gained a little experience in the realm of men, so when the wife dumped him and he was by the side of the road smoking, looking now like an old tubby real uncle, I picked him up in my car and reintroduced myself. I was just out of college and didn't know, in general, what to do with myself, but I paid for the motel and his hands were gentle. He didn't remember me from Beth's time, but he did recall how I had been one of the girls in the scandalous spring musical wearing a giant hat and lingerie. The disappointing part for me was that he didn't appreciate our time together; he seemed to still think of himself as that guy in the movie, and hadn't adjusted to the latest him in the mirror. If you're that good-looking when you're very young, maybe you never really know. I wanted him to be grateful to me for still having a fantasy about him, but he seemed to think I should be grateful to him for deigning to hang out with his niece's friend, and we both left starved for gratitude. We did share some french fries at the motel's diner. Afterward, I dropped him by the side of the road, at his request, and went to the gym.

IAN JAMES
ALLY IN THE POOL, 2012
SILVER GELATIN PRINT
16" x 20"

IAN JAMES
UNTITLED (SPRING SELECTION), 2012
PIGMENT PRINT, 18" X22"

A STRANGER IN SIEM REAP

EVAN JAMES

Over the last decade, I have developed a travel mania. No sooner do I land in one place than I begin to scheme, in the back of my mind, ways of escaping it. I've never taken anything like a proper vacation: every time I board a plane, bus, or train, I'm simply executing one part of an intricate plan to rocket through multiple cities or countries as fast as possible, to burn through all my money immediately, thus returning to a state in which travel is, once more, out of my price range — a state almost as unbearable as traveling itself.

"Plan" is perhaps too strong a word. The travel guru Rick Steves would beat me senseless with a copy of *Asia Through the Back Door* if he saw my most recent itinerary. After a short stint teaching at a university in New Zealand, I had more money than I knew what to do with — over a hundred dollars, I mean — and I decided to blow it on a high-speed, enlightenment-free chase through Southeast Asia.

Halfway through my six-country course, I had already driven a motorbike to a 14th-century Balinese Hindu temple outside Ubud, and haggled over a new tire when I got a flat in an unfamiliar little town. I had spent a few days in the chaotic Indonesian megacity of Jakarta, dancing to American '90s music in a smoke-choked club, clinking beers with an old friend on a high rooftop bar that had, basically, no guardrail, and wandering the almost seven-million-square-foot labyrinth of Grand Indonesia Shopping Town. In the Cambodian capital, I had eaten beef with ant sauce and gone to a baffling drag show. On a shaky Angkor Air flight from Phnom Penh to Siem Reap, I nodded off every few minutes, jolting awake whenever we hit turbulence. Burnout already loomed.

That didn't stop me from noticing a cute passenger across the aisle on my flight to Siem Reap. He looked Arab-ish — born in Iraq, I later learned — and around my age. He spoke French with an attractive Asian woman, his traveling companion. Their intimate laughter reminded me how lonely I was, barreling through the region on my own. After we landed, this pair, Karim and Sylvie, approached me at the baggage claim.

"Excuse me," he said, "but on the plane, we were trying to figure out what you do."

"*Me?*" I was flustered to be seen and commented on. "Well, what did you guess?"

Sylvie hefted a rolling suitcase from the carousel. "I thought cinematographer. Something to do with the image, with composing the scene."

"I was thinking teacher," said Karim. A half-smile suggested mischief — flashing visions, perhaps, of just what kind of lessons I might teach him.

"I wish I was a cinematographer," I said. "But I'm a writer." Saying so felt like oversharing, as if I had confessed a psychological disorder.

The three of us shared a cyclo taxi into town. Karim said he was exhausted, managing, in spite of this, to add flirtatious shading to his words. "I just flew from New York to Shanghai to Phnom Penh to here."

"What *you* need to refresh you," I said, "is an eight-hour, 25-mile off-road mountain bike tour of Angkor Park."

"*Il fait chaud*," said Sylvie, fanning herself. The weather that week hovered around a comfortable 110 degrees. As I hopped off the cyclo at my hotel, they told me they'd think about the mountain bike tour.

They showed up for it the next day. Karim and I, I thought, could certainly fall in love while enduring hours of biking over rough paths, sweating through our shirts, and looking at one galleried Khmer temple after another in potentially lethal heat and humidity. I admired his legs as he pedaled, the hint of chest hair at his drooping collar, the enthusiasm with which he threw himself into this unrelenting expedition. As the afternoon wore on, we took available opportunities to bike side by side, chatting about work, family, travel. He horrified me by saying he had developed a shellfish allergy in his late 20s.

"I ate shrimp, crab, lobster, everything, all through my life," he said. "Then, one evening in New York, I had this huge crab dinner with friends. Within an hour, I started to turn red. My throat closed up, and I had to go to the hospital. I can never eat shellfish again. Who knew it could happen all of a sudden, just like that?"

"Terrifying," I said. "I can't imagine life without lobster." But I was thinking, that yes, one's vulnerabilities can shift in an instant.

A twinkle in his eyes suggested interest dancing behind the encroaching fog of fatigue. I hoped that if I simply continued smiling and asking questions about his life, he'd get the message: I was too tired to sweep him off his feet, so I wished he would sweep me off mine. Whenever he fell back to cycle alongside Sylvie, I hoped that some part of their French conferral concerned me.

Sylvie suffered mild heat stroke toward the end of the tour, nearly fainting, and took a cyclo back to their hotel. As for me and Karim, we found little to say in the final hour, perhaps too concerned with getting to the end in one piece. When will he tell me he really likes me? I thought. When will he tip his hand?

Later that night, I met them for beers, but felt so paralyzed by exhaustion — perhaps he did, too; or by fear masquerading as exhaustion — that we ended up returning to our separate hotels in short order. He was waiting for me, it seemed, to act; I was waiting for him. Normally I don't have this problem, at least when it comes to sex. The pursuit of sex, which is all masks, all theater, requires so little real exposure. What petrified me was that I wanted more than sex from Karim: I longed to fall fully in love with him, which isn't the least bit modern — love demands that you rest in place offstage, endure heroic passages of time together, time in which one must confront, continually, the tired, the ridiculous, the ugly actor behind the role.

I held my face in my hands as the cyclo took me back. I was spending the night alone, again, for fear that love might discover my devouring need of it.

Karim and Sylvie had convinced me to wake up before dawn the next day to see the sun rise over Angkor Wat. Somehow I managed, even though my every instinct howled for me to stay in bed, in hiding. Yet another cyclo carried us through the checkpoint and into the tremendous temple complex. Many other tourists milled about the grounds, taking photographs, buying souvenirs, and wondering aloud whether or not the conditions were right for a really good sunrise. They were. Karim, Sylvie, and I sat on the lawn, bleary-eyed, as the glowing orb of the sun rose, warm, clear, trembling, perfect, touching the tallest spire.

"This really was worth it," said Karim. "Look at that," he said. "*Look!*"

I looked at him, wanting to grab his face with both hands and kiss him. That would have meant to live, though, and in front of all these people. I only played at living.

We spent the rest of the morning exploring the temple grounds in a delirious state, giggling and striking absurd, sometimes lascivious poses in front of statues. I took a photo of Karim and Sylvie in flattering light. "For my mother," he said. Sylvie then took one of me and Karim; I put my arm around him like a friend. A troubling relief came as I felt our hours together fast slipping away.

On the cyclo ride back to town — the last time I'd see him; I slept through the evening, and left the next morning — Karim, unable to stay awake any longer, leaned against me in a doze. The side of his head rested on my shoulder as the rickshaw rumbled over uneven roads. Sylvie, in the opposite seat, her eyes shielded by large sunglasses, smiled, blessing this union — and perhaps still trying to guess my true vocation, even as its comic mask grinned back.

New Moon

CARL ADAMSHICK

Some movie had come out
while my mother was in hospice.
Nurses talked about the lead;
how sexy he was, a saxophonist
in the fifties; wore a sharp suit
with a razor thin tie; gentle
with eyes that kept going.
They showed me how to fold
sheets in such a way
that when I changed them
my mother didn't have to leave
the bed. I wanted to be a nurse.
I wanted to go into houses
and help people dying, which
is what I was doing, except
my mother wasn't a stranger,
she was my mother. And my
family was there, which was
making it easier and much more
difficult. I would heavily salt
fried onions because that is what
she loved. I would take the car
and get her chocolate caramel
explosion malts I didn't want
to give her because that is
what she loved. Her hands
were beautiful. A neighbor's
daughter came and did her nails
a Halloween orange, dyed
her hair, waxed her lip.
My mother told me the summer
she looked best in a two-piece
was 1963. Then apologized
for saying. She was married twice,
each for a span of twenty years.
Each man was my father,
but one of them wasn't.
If I were to be truthful
the movie came out four
months after my mother's
death and they weren't nurses
but friends talking about the lead.
I went to see the movie. It was
beautiful and sad, the choices
and commitments were real
and devastating. The man was sexy,
more a minor character. I did
wish to be alive in black and white
playing a horn like him, my history
stretching back only an hour
to the opening credits where
everything before them collapsed

into nothingness, into no-story,
into something to sleep through,
something to avoid by sleeping.
I'm so thankful she let me be
close to her dying. It was a last
gift, not a gift really, it was how
she took care of me, always
showing me how life is going to be.
My brother, my one brother
who couldn't handle the moon
sliding over our mother's face
took to driving and parking
on the shoulders of highways.
When I watched the movie
and saw the woman walking
back to the convent to maybe
take her vows and become a nun
because outside the cloistered
walls was insane, I thought
of my brother. I wished
he was with me, that we were
watching the movie together
even if the projector didn't
have – didn't have or needed
a bulb. ⁄⁄

THE SIRENS

ROBIN KIRMAN

It's Tuesday evening, July eighth, and my husband, daughter, and I are driving home from an afternoon at the swimming pool. The sun is orange, fading finally; we are nearing the end of another brutally hot day, as summer days in Tel Aviv invariably are. Even at this hour, we must keep the windows up and AC blasting, so that the wailing noise outside is almost too faint to hear. Without my husband beside me, whose ears are alert to the familiar sound of an air raid siren, I might not realize what is happening. A missile, maybe more than one, is heading toward us, rather precisely, since the Israeli military is now able to track the trajectory of missiles so accurately that only the people in the targeted area need to be alerted.

I've never before been in Israel during such an attack. For most of 2012 and 2013, my Israeli husband and I were in the United States, hoping to settle there. Contingency (and a sluggish US economy) has made Israel my home, which means I must learn to maneuver in situations like this one. I must know, as those around me know, what to do when you're driving on a highway in the path of rocket fire.

Under ideal conditions we should pull over and seek shelter — somewhere covered and away from windows or glass. But we're driving south through Holon, on a stretch of highway flanked by mostly empty, neglected land. Land unremarkable but for the fact that more than 60 years ago, in '48, this was the site of deadly clashes between the Haganah and Arabs from the village of Tel Arish. One more example of a history of violence that can, at any moment, erupt into the present.

While the sirens blare we keep on driving into Jaffa; there is a blast overhead, which means, we assume, that the rocket has been intercepted by Israel's missile defense system. That system, the Iron Dome, is the army's great recent achievement: any rocket likely to land in a populated area will be detonated in midair. The success rate, according to the military, is 90 percent — a number that leaves little room for rational fear. As it is, the figures I glimpse through the car window don't look especially afraid. No one is running or shouting; instead, people stand out in the open on street corners and talk soberly into their cellphones. These are faces I know from my neighborhood: shop owners, frequenters of the local café and ice cream shop. Some are Jewish;

some are Arab. Jaffa is home to most of Tel Aviv's Arab population, Christians and Muslims both, a community that typically stands as an example of peaceful coexistence.

Peaceful, if not exactly quiet. When I first moved to Jaffa I was struck by what a noisy place it is — the shouting match that goes on between the church bells and several nearby muezzins. In contrast, the air raid siren here is downright restrained: half as loud as in Holon or Tel Aviv. For me, at first, the sound is easy to miss. It is quite unlike the sirens I know from the States — usually accompanying emergency vehicles — which fluctuate tones, rise and fall in pitch, shift their rhythm, and follow the path of their source. Israel's military siren seems to come from nowhere in particular. It is a single held note, solemn, even plaintive.

From within Jaffa, if you happen to be inside, listening for news on the radio or running the dishwasher or fan, you might not hear the warning signal altogether. This puts our neighborhood at greater risk. I ask my husband how such an oversight can happen — if this is an example of lesser concern for Arab lives. But no, nothing as sinister as that: the reason (implicitly understood, though never publicly acknowledged) is that the same alarm that functions during a live attack is also used to commemorate Israel's Holocaust Remembrance Day and Memorial Day. The latter is the most solemn day of the year in this country — painful, in a different way, for the Arab-Israeli community. It would be offensive for the state to blast its siren here, so the low volume is an instance of the sort of unremarked compromise that makes life in this place possible.

As far as my family's security is concerned, the siren's low volume is a disadvantage; where its emotional welfare is concerned, it's a gift. Thankfully, my daughter doesn't need to be terrified by shrieking alarms. When we do notice the sound, we calmly gather in her nursery — there is no official safe room in our house, so my daughter's room, bounded by the thickest walls, will have to do. We play songs for her while the bombs explode. We feel relief that she will not be — so far — scarred like the children in the barraged towns along the southern border: children who, the papers report, wake screaming at night and cry while their houses shake.

The way we experience this conflict in Jaffa is nothing like families in places like Ashkelon or Ashdod, and obviously incomparable to the horrors suffered in Gaza, which the IDF has already begun shelling. To have an inkling of what these others are suffering, we consult the news: my husband follows the Israeli press, and I follow the American. In the Times and elsewhere, the images out of Gaza are of bodies lifted from rubble, mothers wailing at the funerals of their sons. Across the border, on the Israeli side, there's almost nothing for a photographer to capture: faint plumes of smoke from detonated missiles, onlookers gathered around charred pieces of debris. An article in *Bloomberg* states that the absence of Israeli losses makes the Iron Dome a military triumph and a PR disaster: the system functions too well, and so becomes an infuriating symbol of the unfairness of the fight. Another article, in *The Atlantic*, suggests that the efficacy of the system has been widely exaggerated. Here and elsewhere I encounter avid speculation that, for various motives — controlling the local population, increasing profits in Israeli arms sales — the military is conducting an elaborate air show.

If Americans take such debates seriously, the population here does not. There's no need to consult pollsters or talking heads to gauge the public's confidence in the military's capability. One just needs to step outside. Cars are driving on the road; businesses are open; restaurants are full. The scene in Tel Aviv is almost unaffected — not the case, my husband tells me, before the Iron

Dome was implemented. During similar attacks in the '90s, he recalls a deserted city, residents either fleeing to join friends and family in the north, or remaining sequestered in their homes. The phenomenal achievement of this technology isn't merely that it prevents civilian deaths. It allows most Israelis to exist in a condition of perpetual conflict and yet go about their lives.

One can be critical of such a solution, naturally. Were more Israelis dying, perhaps the drive to seek peace would be more urgent and perhaps fewer Palestinian lives would be lost as a result. The opposite argument might also be made: ground invasions of Gaza would be called for more readily and frequently, and the death toll would be even greater. Such questions, however significant, grow rather abstract when you are hiding with your baby daughter in her nursery, awaiting the next sequence of explosions and hoping one of these will not be among the 10 percent of rockets that won't be intercepted. Some here, Jews, Christians, and Muslims, pray to their gods in such moments; others, like me, find it easier to stake our faith in this other unseen, mysterious intelligence that guards us from above.

Almost a week passes this way. On average, there are about two sirens per day, two occasions when my family huddles together, waiting for the blasts. Sometimes these are faint; sometimes they seem to shake the walls of our stone house. Between these incidents, we stick to our usual routine but with slight modifications. At night, we sleep without a fan; we do the dishes by hand and only play my daughter's games and songs at a low volume. (Keeping the house quiet is hardly the sort of accommodation I'd expect to make during a rocket attack.) In the morning, we drop my daughter at her *gan* (daycare or kindergarten). Only now, when we ride in the car, we listen to the radio to hear updates on the latest injuries and deaths. After the reports, peace songs from the '70s are played; my daughter rocks to the beat in her car seat.

My daughter's school is closed only once in this first week of bombings, and then, by mistake. Hamas has sent out a public message impersonating the IDF and warning of a massive strike against Gaza scheduled for noon that day. Israeli citizens are advised to remain near shelters. Half an hour after the message has gone out, the IDF announces that it was a hoax, but by then the nervous teachers at my daughter's school (as elsewhere, no doubt) have already sent the children home. Events like this don't make the news in the US, overshadowed — probably rightfully — by bloodier aspects of the conflict. But rumors and misinformation are also part of Hamas's strategy, an attempt to unsettle the population and interfere with the progress of everyday existence.

Many Israelis seem to feel, therefore, that it is a patriotic duty to remain responsibly undaunted by the threat. If my daughter's classroom is half empty, this is only because she attends a fancy gan in Neve Tzedek, where half the parents are American and European. If the boardwalk and beaches by our house are less crowded, this is because the tourists have stopped coming. The other figures notably absent are the Israeli Arabs, who otherwise visit from Judea and Samaria on the weekends. This is a relatively recent phenomenon: the cheering sight of thousands of Arabs who feel comfortable enough to spend Friday evenings and Saturdays on the beach between Tel Aviv and Jaffa. The men cooking barbecues and smoking nargiles on the lawn; the women wading out into the surf in their headscarves and their robes.

As my husband and I take our evening walks along the shore, I wonder if those who stay home are right to, and if we are being foolishly brazen putting ourselves, and our child, in danger. My husband isn't one to display fear; he served in the military as a Navy SEAL, and though he's

RADENKO MILAK, *BIG TIME*, 2013
WATERCOLOR ON PAPER
50 X 65 CENTIMETERS
COURTESY GALLERY DUPLEX 100M^2 AND L'AGENCE À PARIS

extremely cynical about his homeland, his patriotism can sometimes emerge with sudden and stubborn force. I convince myself that it is a relatively small chance we are taking: the only real risk is from falling debris. Near our home in Jaffa, this risk is slightly greater. Given the path of the rockets from Gaza into Tel Aviv, and the point of interception by Israel's defensive missiles, Jaffa happens to be where much of the debris lands. As we proceed, my husband points out locations we should run for if the siren sounds: a picnic table, a bench. At one point a car door slams and I think I hear a bomb. A few minutes later I do hear a bomb, an actual explosion, and peer up, hoping to catch a flash of fire or trail of smoke, traces in the sky.

Tuesday morning, July 15, I awake to news of a cease-fire. I let myself believe that the conflict is over, at least until the next event triggers hostilities again. That afternoon I hear no alarms or explosions; I get no frantic calls from my daughter's teachers. It's only later in the day that I hear the agreement has collapsed and that Hamas and then Israel have resumed their assaults. I am upset and disappointed — no doubt naively, from the perspective of those who've endured the same frustrations so often before. Exactly one week has elapsed since the first rocket fire into Tel Aviv, hundreds of innocents in Gaza have been killed, and yet it seems we are just where we started. My family and I are once again driving home from Holon at sunset when we hear the alarm.

This time we are already in Jaffa, close to home. A restaurant stands open across the street and so we run for shelter there. On the way, my daughter observes a row of pigeons perched along a telephone wire: "birds," she says, using one of her newly acquired words. She is excited to enter the restaurant, where music is playing and where she dances to the amusement of the waitresses. The music is too loud for us to hear the blast, but, through the window, I see those birds along the wire dart off frantically.

After a few moments we thank the staff and head back home. I go inside to prepare my daughter's dinner; my husband stays outside, watering the cactus plants we keep instead of grass. He's standing over our approximated lawn when a neighbor comes by. The neighbor believes he heard something crashing through the tree above our house. It might be a cat — Jaffa is rife with strays — but best we check things out.

My husband and the neighbor are already up on the roof, marveling at the object, when I join them. On a pile of leaves sits a piece of shining metal. It's more than just a fragment of debris, as I expect to find. It is about the size of a soccer ball, shaped like a dome; wires extrude from the broken end. This cannot be part of any rocket from Gaza, where only crude weapons are available, so even I, whose understanding of such things is also crude, quickly understand what I am seeing: the head of an Iron Dome missile, nestled in the leaves just above our living room.

My husband calls the police who arrive within 10 minutes, and who, in turn, call the appropriate military unit. As we are waiting, my husband and our neighbor reconstruct the event from the clues around us: the fresh leaves from where the fragment fell through the tree branches above; the three-inch-wide indentation where it first hit the roof; a chip on a side wall where it ricocheted and then landed on the pile where it now rests. Meanwhile, the policemen stand around and gape; they've never seen anything like this before, not in person or in the news, where such a large, important section of the missile would never be permitted to be shown. Another neighbor, walking past, observes the gathering up on the roof and comes to see what is the matter.

Fascinated by the rocket, he takes out his phone to snap a picture. The policemen shout at him to stop. This is a secret object, the brain of one of the world's most intelligent missiles. I'm told not to get too close and, of course, not to touch.

When the military arrives 20 minutes later, the sun has set and the roof is dark. They shine a flashlight on the spot and lift the piece with their bare hands. From the doorway of my kitchen, with my daughter in my arms, I watch them haul the thing away, down the dim stone alleyway outside our house.

Three days later, my family and I board a plane headed for New York. We've scheduled this visit many months ago; the violence hasn't affected our plans, though I must admit I feel relief to be getting out when I am. (Coincidentally, our flight leaves the same evening that the ground invasion of Gaza begins.) From here on, when I encounter the mounting bloodshed in the region, it is, more or less, as an American again: watching the awful stories on *NewsHour* and *Charlie Rose*, never worrying if the TV is playing too loudly to hear a faint alarm sounding outside.

When friends express their concern about my family's welfare, when they ask if we've been frightened, I'm quick to reassure them. This is a war that has gone on above our heads. Unlike those in Gaza, and unlike the Israeli soldiers then dying on the ground, we have confronted it as history. By the time it hits us, in fragments, we experience it as a kind of archaeology. We are lucky to be touched by the violence so lightly — lightly, and yet so very close. For the next days and weeks, I hear echoes of bombs with every slammed door or backfiring car. I think too about the fact that we will soon be returning home, where my daughter's nursery can, at any moment, become again a safe room. And where the roof, when I come up to survey the still-strange view from my house, will be the spot where a chunk of metal landed after saving the lives of Jews and Arabs both, those Israelis who have become my neighbors.

MY ONLY UNCLE

MONA SIMPSON

My Uncle was a salesman. When I was a small child, he held the local franchise of a national firm and won prizes for selling the most water softeners in the state of Wisconsin and then in the upper Midwestern region, prizes which allowed him to take his family to faraway vacations in Disneyland in California, the Everglades in Florida, and the Bahamas. My own tiny family, if you could call it that — we were only two — didn't take vacations, though for years my mother talked about visiting the Wisconsin Dells and Baraboo, where the Ringling Brothers Circus was said to winter.

Later, my Uncle owned his own businesses, selling soap, the Rug Doctor, and vitamins, and the building in which he housed his stock on the east side of Green Bay at a location called Three Corners.

He'd always supported his wife and two sons. If my aunt ever worked it was "at the store," which meant that she helped out by doing the books in the business. But that work never interfered with her card days or her lunches with members of the birthday club. My own mother, those years, was always dashing, late to a school out of town, in Suamico or Pulaski, carrying a stack of manila files that threatened to topple and sometimes did.

My Uncle was considered a big spender, splurging on presents he was famous in the family for buying the very afternoon of Christmas Eve. On ordinary weekday mornings, he went out to Bob's Big Boy for breakfast and ordered coffee and toast. "As if he couldn't have toast at home," my grandmother would mutter.

Jerry came from a large Catholic Green Bay family with many sisters and brothers. One of his sisters worked at the airport. Another made Christmas tree decorations out of Styrofoam and velvet ribbons. Those two never married. My cousins had lots of cousins, aunts, and uncles. My mother had only one sister. We had only them.

Their family was gregarious. They owned a snowmobile, a boat, and a trailer; they camped at a lake where they did water sports, and in winter they skied. My oldest cousin broke an arm once during vacation at Pine Mountain, and after a week moping around bored he skied with his cast in a sling and then broke a leg too.

My earliest memories of my aunt and uncle are set in vibrant adult social life with friends. My aunt wore full-skirted dresses and pointed high heels and laughed with a high tinkling sound.

"Oh, Jerry," I remember her saying, sitting on his lap.

And yet there was nothing merry about him. He was fearsome, to all of us.

I don't think I ever talked to him alone. I'd grown up with my mother and my grandmother; I wasn't used to men. With two sons, he wasn't used to little girls either. And my mother was a character to him. She'd gone to college and graduate school and married a foreign professor who was now who knows where. She was too proud of her MA degree for him. Neither my aunt nor my uncle had gone past high school.

For decades, even as an adult, it never occurred to me to consider my Uncle's accomplishments or to imagine that he had been proud of them, though all the evidence was there, spread out before me. He added onto the house he and my aunt built when they were married, on a large lot next door to my grandmother's. He constructed a wing he called "the breezeway" by himself and, several times redid the large patio in the backyard, eventually putting in a swimming pool. Before he retired, he owned his Green Bay home, a house in Florida, and the building at Three Corners where he'd run his businesses. Those properties now support his oldest son.

I loved my aunt and my cousins, but I never accorded my Uncle the respect he deserved and, perhaps as a result we weren't close. My mother's friends were oddballs: a spinster who'd gone to college and then come back to work at the *Press-Gazette*, young Jesuit priests from St. Norbert College, a couple in which the mother was a new paper photographer and the father a lawyer who made sculptures in the backyard. In sixth grade we read *Death of A Salesman*.

But my Uncle was not Willy Loman. He had no mortgages and bought everything outright, when possible with cash.

My aunt and uncle retired to Florida, where they lived on a compound with a golf course. When my first novel came out, I asked my publisher to include a trip to Naples on the book tour. My aunt worked with an independent bookstore, which mainly sold crystals. I was their first visiting author. When I arrived a nine-foot-high float had been made for me to ride in, with tissue paper stuffed in chicken wire to look like my book jacket.

By then, already, my Uncle was losing parts of his mind. He would ask his wife to put on and take off his shirt 10 times in an hour, shouting. She was always soft-voiced with him, saying, "Oh, Jerry."

My Uncle Jerry was a successful man. This was something I never understood while he was alive and, in fact may have been the reason that he hated me, a condition I always assumed, though I had no particular proof. He'd never hit me, as he'd hit his own children. He was not especially mean. His voice had something like a minatory growl in it, but I think he spoke that way to everyone.

My own parents had not stayed married. My father didn't keep in touch at all. When it was time for me to go to college, I didn't even have an address at which to contact him, to ask for help. And yet some misguided loyalty to my own kept me from bothering with my only Uncle at all.

For years and years I had a memory that wasn't real. I was staying home in a living room with a bay window, configured unlike any house I'd ever lived in. A quiet room, with an old person sitting somewhere behind. They were packing the station wagon to go on a trip. My close cousin kept coming to say goodbye to me.

I stood next to a table set with doilies and African violets, watching the red car outside, being loaded in the bright sunlight.

GINA MARIE NAPOLITAN, *HOUSE OF REST*
MIXED MEDIA ON WATERCOLOR PAPER

The Big Sleep #2

MARTHA RONK

> *The blue carpet darkened a shade or two and the walls drew back into remoteness. The chairs filled with shadowy loungers. In the corners were memories like cobwebs.*

Expanse of blue carpet scuffed up a dusty whiff of it
from the still air of the street to the still air of a complex
where anyone's been before,
                    the entryway to a hunch.

Architecture's the map of mystery, the uncertainty of an elevator,
its momentary glitch. Somewhere beyond the door is somewhere
to get to.

                    Stalled, the first paragraph of a chapter
describes the foyer, the furniture and some indescribable emptiness-
the weight of the unplotted,
                    the material stuff of astonishment.

> *Inside, in the square barren lobby, a man put a green evening paper down beside a potted palm and flicked a cigarette butt into the tub the palm grew in.*

The startle not of blackmail, but of *the green evening news*. Since when.
Another mystery, another time.

Murder's in the details.

THE EVERGREEN DREAM

ALICE BOLIN

I had lived in Los Angeles for six months when I starting spending long hours in its cemeteries, drawn to them like a self-pitying moth to a lonely, maudlin flame. I still only had one friend in the city; I had expansive free time and no direction and no prospects. From the beginning, I had trouble reconciling my daily experience of Los Angeles — as a young and changing city; as green and mountainous; as an incredibly ethnically diverse city, with a culture and population that is predominantly Latino — with the sun-bleached, suburban sprawl-y, valley girlish, cultureless, entertainment-industry-glamorous idea I had of it before I moved here. Could these images coexist, both taking some share of the truth?

I would walk from my apartment in Koreatown a mile and a half north to Santa Monica Boulevard to the strange oasis of Hollywood Forever Cemetery, 60 acres in the middle of East Hollywood backing onto the Paramount lot, land Paramount bought, in fact, from Hollywood Forever in the early 20th century, when it was still Hollywood Memorial Park Cemetery. Hollywood Forever is a tourist destination, famous for housing stars like Rudolph Valentino, John Huston, Estelle Getty, and two of the Ramones. Legendary director Cecil B. DeMille is buried with his wife, Constance, in a pair of giant Arthurian tombs. Tyrone Power's grave quotes from *Hamlet* — the "Goodnight, sweet prince" speech, naturally.

But the fancy pedigree of a few of its inhabitants is not immediately apparent on entering. Hollywood Forever contains a historic Jewish burial ground, Beth Olam, and the rows of monuments with non-famous Jewish names and Stars of David were the first ones I noticed. The cemetery is very close to LA's Little Armenia, and there are large sections of Armenian names with etchings of the dead in their Sunday best staring from the graves unnervingly. Many of the monuments are truly old, from before the birth of a Los Angeles motion picture industry, from when Los Angeles meant something completely different.

At times my eye would catch on a large or ornate monument — this is irritating because it is what these graves are designed to do; the rich exercising their control even after death — or a famous name, but the overall feeling in Hollywood Forever is not like gawking down the Hollywood Walk of Fame. As in most cemeteries, chaos reigns in Hollywood Forever — the graves go in every direction, so crowded in some places that they give the sense that they are in storage, jumbled together until they are moved to their real plots. Peacocks swagger around the grounds, indifferent to visitors. Quirky and beautiful, Hollywood Forever is more than the celebrity it is known for, in the same way that Los Angeles is.

Jules Roth, the crook owner of Hollywood Memorial from 1939 until his death in 1998, allowed it to fall into shameful disrepair, its crematorium forced to shut down in 1974 after the botched cremation of Mama Cass Elliot. In 1998, two young developers, Tyler and Brent Cassity, bought Hollywood Memorial and rebranded it as Hollywood Forever, focusing on making a center for cultural programs like concerts and summer movies, where the audience scans itself for famous faces, where before the film the audience can seek out famous names in the confused rows of graves.

But is that what it's *about*? Is Hollywood Forever about celebrity, is it about Los Angeles Judaism, about its ethnic enclaves, about the city's turn-of-the-century oligarchy? Does this depend on which iteration of the cemetery you believe — the bankrupt, shambolic Hollywood Memorial or the hip and cultured Hollywood Forever? Do these distinctions even apply? As with everything in Los Angeles, I'm learning, objects in the mirror are always closer than they appear.

Forest Lawn Memorial Park in Glendale is spacious and sprawling — five times the size of Hollywood Forever — self-styled as an English country estate. I've only been there once, on a freak 100-degree day in April. When I entered its wrought-iron gates — the largest in the world, Forest Lawn claims — I saw rolling hills of grass furling from the main drive. As I approached, I was startled by the rows of bronze plaques against the green. That is what Forest Lawn is designed to be: the kind of cemetery where one is surprised by graves.

I walked the grounds for an hour, wandering through the cemetery's oldest graves, many of them bulky and embellished, from before the bronze markers were enforced. I visited the park's walled gardens, also filled with graves, and its specialized sections — Babyland the most chilling. It is true that many of the 20th century's greatest stars are buried at Forest Lawn, but they aren't luring tourists like at Hollywood Forever: Michael Jackson, Clark Gable, and Jean Harlow are all memorialized in elite sections of the cemetery's mausoleum that are not open to the public. I was so overwhelmed by Forest Lawn's scale and the day's heat that I staggered straight from the cemetery to an Atwater Village bar, makeup and sunscreen streaking down my face.

As Ben Ehrenreich writes in a masterly 2010 *Los Angeles* magazine feature, an exhaustive investigation of the business of dying in LA, "Los Angeles holds a special place in the history of death." This is largely because of the fascination (and awe, and disgust) Forest Lawn has elicited in its visitors. From the time it was acquired in 1912 by Dr. Hubert Eaton — known as "The Builder" — it was designed to be "as unlike other cemeteries as sunshine is unlike darkness." Eschewing the chaotic development of most cemeteries, the concept for Forest Lawn sprang fully formed from Eaton's imagination: the replicas of English churches and reproductions of da Vinci's sculptures, and the zoning, "a rigid real estate hierarchy," says Ehrenreich, "that reflects L.A.'s own." This is integral to Forest Lawn's business model, as it manufactures a demand for plots in certain areas of the park and so justifies their exorbitant price tags.

One of Forest Lawn's most enthusiastic and horrified explorers was the English novelist Evelyn Waugh, who called it "a completely unique place — the only thing in California that is not a copy of something else." (Never mind all of the architectural and artistic imitation within.) Waugh came to Hollywood in 1947 to develop a script for an adaptation of his novel *Brideshead Revisited* for MGM Studios. He found the motion picture industry and the United States generally to be completely distasteful, but he took perverse pleasure in learning about Forest Lawn — "morticians [...] are the *only* people worth knowing," he wrote to a friend — and the American funeral industry. His short novel about Forest Lawn, *The Loved One*, is one of the most brutal and hilarious satires ever written about American culture.

Waugh invents the engineering marvel of Kaiser's Stoneless Peaches, which taste to *The Loved One*'s British poet hero, Dennis Barlow, like "a ball of damp, sweet, cotton-wool." Waugh adds, "Kaiser's radio half-hour brought Wagner into every kitchen." He writes endlessly of the convenience and indistinguishability of American women, so that they seem to be manifest from the same American mania for mass production. Dennis wonders as he stares at a woman's leg, "Which came first in this strange civilization, [...] the foot or the shoe, the leg or the nylon stocking?"

Forest Lawn — or as Waugh fictionalized it, Whispering Glades — is a pure and disturbing expression of this American sterility and consumerism. Waugh mimics Forest Lawn's relentlessly positive and euphemistic corporate language. The Builder is figured in *The Loved One* as "The Dreamer." "Let me explain the Dream" is how the Mortuary Hostess, "one of that new race of exquisite, amiable, efficient young ladies" who populate the United States, begins her discussion of funeral arrangements with Dennis. Corpses are known as "Loved Ones," as when a makeup artist says to an embalmer, "Here is the strangulated Loved One for the Orchid Room."

Waugh was particularly appalled by the prevalence of embalming at Forest Lawn — that is, the draining of a corpse's bodily fluids and its preservation with formaldehyde — which, as Ehrenreich points out, "is practiced nowhere else in the world with the near universality that it achieved in North America." Waugh writes in his 1947 essay "Half in Love with Easeful Death" about the premodern handling of death in Europe, a tradition that was full of reminders that the body is impermanent, "a marble skeleton lurking somewhere among the marble draperies and quartered escutcheons of the tombs of the high renaissance." For Waugh, embalming nullified any memento mori, as "the body does not decay; it lives on, more chic in death than ever before, in its indestructible class A steel and concrete shelf." This was the true horror of Forest Lawn: its cheery but enfeebled idea of death, one designed to appeal to the American capitalist. "Dr. Eaton is the first man to offer eternal salvation at an inclusive charge as part of his undertaking service," wrote Waugh.

But America in *The Loved One* is not only consumerist and unnatural; it is also dispossessed. Waugh is conscious of the ethnic diversity of American names as remnants of identities lost — there are characters named Otto Baumbein and Lorenzo Medici, Miss Mavrocordato and Mr. Van Gluck. Barlow's American paramour, a cosmetician at Whispering Glades, is named Aimée Thanatogenos, which, if my French and Greek serve me, can be roughly translated as "The Loved One." Aimée is Waugh's quintessential American orphan, named, by unreliable parents, after legendary Los Angeles televangelist Aimee Semple McPherson.

In Waugh's novel the US is depicted as a land of transients, shorn of their previous identities and their history. Dennis is a World War II veteran, and he "came of a generation which enjoys a vicarious intimacy with death." He is presumably drawn to Whispering Glades, however unwillingly, because it displays that same intimacy, a brazen comfort with death. Ehrenreich describes, in contrast, how 19th-century Europeans rejected the earlier familiarity and visibility of death in their culture, making it something "shameful and forbidden." One reason Europeans continue to be so dumbfounded by Forest Lawn is its spectacular resistance to the modern Western trend of making death and its reminders smaller, less grand, more separate from society. In Waugh's depiction, Forest Lawn effaces death in other ways: by stopping the effects of decay, by simplifying ideas of the afterlife. But Forest Lawn is still "a necropolis of the age of the Pharaohs," as Waugh wrote in "Half in Love with Easeful Death," "created in the middle of the impious twentieth century." Perhaps Forest Lawn reflects American identity not only in its capitalist model, but also in a comfort with death that reflects the two violent and contradictory centuries of the United States' existence.

I was wandering Hollywood Forever again when I discovered the corner of the park dedicated to the Otis-Chandler family, the legendary owners of the *Los Angeles Times*. Harrison Gray Otis, the first successful publisher of the paper, is buried beneath a mammoth obelisk. His son-in-law and heir, Harry Chandler, gets a curving marble slab flanked with urns and a pair of bald eagles. And among the rosebushes and religious statues shading the Otis-Chandler graves, I found a disconcerting monument, another large marble structure topped with a bronze sculpture of an eagle perched on its aerie, preparing for flight. "OUR MARTYRED MEN" reads the adorning plaque, in memory of the men who "fell at their posts in The Times Building on the awful morning of October first, 1910 — victims of conspiracy, dynamite and fire — The Crime of the Century."

The what?

I had never heard about the *LA Times* bombing of 1910, in which 21 of the paper's employees, "defenders of Industrial Freedom under Law," as the plaque at Hollywood Forever puts it, were killed by a bomb planted by the Structural Iron Workers union. Neither had anyone I informally surveyed after my discovery: my mother, father, brothers, or boyfriend. I was perplexed that my entire education, which includes, for what it's worth, a bachelor's degree in history, had neglected a terrorist attack on a major US newspaper, an attack so traumatic that it had once been considered "the crime of the century." But it is starting to seem fitting to me that I only found evidence of this trauma in Hollywood Forever. Monuments do not only serve to help us remember; they also allow us to forget and move on.

Curiosity led me to Howard Blum's 2008 book *American Lightning*, an enjoyable but irritating nonfiction novel about the *LA Times* attack. It tracks three American icons as they converged at Downtown Los Angeles's Alexandria Hotel at the time of the bombing: Billy Burns, the "American Sherlock Holmes," later famous for his part in the Teapot Dome cover-up, whose agency tracked down the bombers, J.J. McNamara and his brother Jim; Clarence Darrow, the great populist attorney, who defended the McNamaras; and D. W. Griffith, the father of American cinema, as he made the first moves to establish the Los Angeles entertainment industry. The most interesting parts of the book are the chronicles of Burns's and his operatives' remarkable (and for Burns, characteristically illegal) detective work. Burns connected bomb sites in Los Angeles and Illinois, tracked a suspect using a pile of sawdust, trailed suspects for months in an anarchist colony on Puget Sound and the forests of Wisconsin, used the first "bug" to listen in on jailhouse conversations, kidnapped and tortured witnesses, and extrajudicially extradited the McNamaras to California.

American Lightning is compelling because of its details — its description of Darrow's Chicago apartment, or the ship Griffith sought out for his film *Enoch Arden*, or the movie a Burns operative watched while on a stakeout — which make it a completely realized narrative. Its failure is in the shallow conclusions it draws from the events it recreates so vividly. The *Times* attack was the most dramatic in the Structural Iron Workers' massive bombing campaign, in which they dynamited over a hundred scab sites all over the United States — they sought to economically devastate Harrison Gray Otis, the paper's fervently antiunion publisher. Blum asserts that the McNamara trial ended the war between capital and labor, and "helped to move America into the modern world." "Entrepreneurial opportunities took shape," he writes breezily, "and they spread through the nation's cities and towns as a more hopeful alternative to the desperation of violence." Blum's optimistic, restorative reading of the situation is even more bizarre considering that the bombing occurred almost exactly 100 years before the crime of *this* century, and the two events bear a ghostly similarity.

In Blum's description of labor terrorism and the McNamaras' trial, he must be drawing a conscious connection to the problems of our contemporary War on Terror. When Burns kidnapped and illegally transported the McNamaras across state lines, ignoring habeas corpus, his reasons were startlingly familiar: "the nation, [Burns] believed, was 'fighting a war against terrorists' who were determined to destroy 'the established form of government of this country.'" And many invoked the rules of war to defend the McNamaras. An editorial written by newspaper publisher E. W. Scripps insisted that,

> If belligerent rights were accorded to the two parties in this war, then McNamara was guilty of no greater offense than would be the officer of any band, large or small, of soldiers who ordered his men to fire upon an enemy and killed a great number of them.

These questions — about the legal status of terrorists and whether to classify terrorism as a crime or as an act of war — were not, as Blum seems to suggest, problems that had to be worked through in order to thrust the United States into modernity. They exactly prefigured the murkiness of modern warfare and the extreme violence of the 20th century. Blum takes a similar, strangely uncomplicated view of Griffith's masterpiece, *Birth of a Nation*, which he claims "would help America — its art, its ideals, its imagination — move into the modern world." He doesn't attempt to reconcile this with his understanding of the film as regressive and disturbing, "an odd, sour, and disturbingly racist reinterpretation of the Civil War and Reconstruction." With his Panglossian perspective on "modern America," he sidesteps, without exactly ignoring, the injuries and atrocities that loom beneath the faceless ideals of freedom and progress.

Blum's picture of 20th-century America, which is primarily ideal and secondarily actual, finds a unique reflection in Los Angeles, the quintessential 20th-century city. Much of *American Lightning* focuses on Otis, the publisher who helped to transform "a drab mud and adobe town of 11,000" in 1882 into a metropolitan center whose population was 900,000 at the time of the bombing. Otis was, as Mike Davis writes in his serialized biography of the publisher, *The Ghost of Wrath*, "the most hated man in Ragtime America," with "his enemies ecumenically [spanning] a spectrum from evangelists to citrus growers, socialists to robber barons." He figured himself as a military leader, calling himself "the General" and his house "the Bivouac," leading a campaign of mini–manifest destiny that included Los Angeles annexing San Pedro and Wilmington in order to create its port.

Joan Didion, in "Times Mirror Square," her 1990 investigation of the history of the *Los Angeles Times*, writes how Otis and his descendants exerted tremendous influence, using the *Times* as a platform not only to champion the growth of the city but also to increase their personal wealth. Didion describes how the development of Downtown LA and the San Fernando Valley, the creation of the Southern California aerospace industry, the founding of Cal Tech, the hosting of the 1932 Olympics, the making of the Hollywood Bowl, and the building of the freeway system were all undertaken because of the "impulse to improve Chandler property."

"The extent to which Los Angeles was literally invented by the *Los Angeles Times* and by its owners [...] remains hard for people in less recent parts of the country to fully apprehend," Didion writes. This is a city begotten from an idea, as Forest Lawn was begotten from the mind of The Builder, and it relies heavily on the idea to sustain it. The founding idea, the dream of limitless growth, is intertwined with the city's most troubling attributes — its sprawl, its lack of natural resources. This is why all true explorations of the Los Angeles condition express, as Didion writes, "how fragile the idea of the place was and how easily it could be lost."

Early in *American Lightning*, Billy Burns describes a juicy theory of the *Los Angeles Times* bombing. It deals with the scheme to divert water from the Owens River Valley on the Nevada border 250 miles to Los Angeles. Los Angeles voters, after much passionate goading from the *Times*, had approved $22.5 million in bonds to fund the creation of the aqueduct, but at the time of the bombings, Harrison Gray Otis was about to double down on a water scheme that would make him and his business partners millions.

Otis and his partners, using the front of the Los Angeles Suburban Homes Company, had been buying and developing cheap land in the desert stretches of the San Fernando Valley, north of LA. They would use water from the Owens Aqueduct to make the Valley habitable. But their plan had encountered obstacles: the aqueduct was still not finished, and citizens would have to approve more bonds for its completion. Additionally, the Socialist party was gaining traction with Los Angeles voters, and they disapproved of, as one of them said, "handing the aqueduct water over to the land barons"; if Socialists prevailed in the 1911 mayoral election, Otis and the Suburban Homes Company would have no water for the homes they had spent so much to build in the Valley.

Burns proposes that Otis himself was behind the bombing of the *Times* building. He had recently taken out a large insurance policy on the *Times* building, money that would help buoy him while the aqueduct was completed. And by blaming labor for the bombing, he would tarnish the reputation of their Socialist allies, ruining their chances in the 1911 elections.

This was wrong, as it turns out. The McNamaras were behind the attacks, and they did hurt the Socialists' place in Los Angeles politics, handing Otis his goal of a developed San Fernando Valley, a testament to his good luck. Still, it makes an irresistible story, a solution Blum probably would have chosen for his mystery if he hadn't been constrained by fact. It has the hallmarks of a classic noir tale, all of which take place in cities where corruption is the rule, not an aberration. The only thing the story lacks is the noir impulse to, as Faye Dunaway memorably says in 1974's *Chinatown*, "*cherchez la femme*."

Chinatown, one of the masterpiece mysteries in film history, is a noir-ification of the plot to bring Owens River water to Los Angeles. In the film, the chief engineer at the Los Angeles Department of Water and Power, Hollis Mulwray, is murdered after he publicly opposes plans to build a reservoir. Private detective Jake Gittes (Jack Nicholson channeling Philip Marlowe), working with Mulwray's wife, Evelyn (Dunaway), uncovers a complicated plot by Mulwray's former partner and Evelyn's father, Noah Cross, to buy up land in the San Fernando Valley using the names of senile retirees and to covertly and illegally irrigate it using Los Angeles's water.

In the film's ending, it trades a noir aesthetic for a gothic one — Cross is a true villain who has raped Evelyn and fathered her daughter. Evelyn, as it turns out, is not a femme fatale; the film's surprise is in how tightly the apparent system of power holds fast, how straightforward allegiances are, and how little our heroes can do in the face of corrupt authority. Melodramatic as it is, *Chinatown* is a weirdly apt depiction of a city that was developed by a handful of powerful men who did not have much use for rules or ethics.

In *American Lightning*, Blum writes about the early triumph of Griffith's short film *A Corner in Wheat*. It featured an ambitious parallel structure, following "farmers stoically working in a field; the Wheat King hatching his plot to control the market; and the city's downtrodden poor hoping to buy bread," sending a poignant message about the power imbalance in the relationship between America's land owners, producers, and consumers. The film is based on *The Pit* (1903), the second novel in what Frank Norris planned as an epic trilogy (Norris died before completing the third) that began with *The Octopus* (1901) — a true California story that, in California fashion, is more complicated than the patterns *A Corner in Wheat* would distill from it.

In her 2003 meditation on California identity, *Where I Was From*, Didion spends significant time trying to make sense of *The Octopus*. On its surface, it is an anti-corporate novel about the megalithic power of the railroad to control and abuse the humble farmer. A pivotal scene involves a shootout between ranchers in the San Joaquin Valley and federal marshals hired by the Southern Pacific railroad to evict them. There are also scenes where a poet, who writes of the plight of the poor farmer, eats in the opulent domain of the Railroad King while one of the ranchers' widow and daughters fall into degradation and prostitution, and another in which the poet throws an anarchist bomb himself, although his capitalist target is unscathed.

But these conflicts are not as allegorical as they may appear. Crucially, these ranchers were, as Didion writes, "in no sense simple farmers"; they were entrepreneurs who had come to California seeking a fortune from its fecundity in the same way gold rush spectators had tried to exploit its mineral resources, and their business plans were dependent on their proximity to railroad routes. "The only actual conflict in *The Octopus*," Didion writes, "turns out to be between successful and failed members of the same entrepreneurial class." This recalls incestuous themes in *Chinatown*, as parties that seem to be opponents are in fact closely aligned. The development of Southern California followed no traditional narratives; it was uniquely intentional, flowing from a singular energy, serving the interests of a certain small population of men, whether Harrison Gray Otis, Noah Cross, or the Railroad King.

But the infighting among these men is a distraction from what has always been the real story. As Didion succinctly explains,

> *The Octopus* is not, as it might logically seem to be, a story of an agrarian society overtaken by the brute momentum of industrialization: the octopus, if there is one, turns out to be neither the railroad nor corporate ownership but indifferent nature.

This was what Burns knew when devising his theory that the *LA Times* bombing was an inside job. In Los Angeles, the imperative is not to *cherchez la femme*; it is to *cherchez* the water.

The Octopus begins on a day when "all the vast reaches of the San Joaquin Valley — in fact all South Central California, was bone dry, parched, and baked and crisped after four months of cloudless weather." More than a century later, this description bears down on the San Joaquin like a death sentence. A May 30, 2014 *Los Angeles Times* feature describes how extreme drought conditions have devastated families of migrant farm workers. Waves of farmers fled to California from Oklahoma, Texas, Missouri, and Arkansas during the disastrous droughts of the 1930s; now farm workers are migrating away from Southern California's own dust bowl. Communities in the San Joaquin are fading, in danger of becoming ghost towns. "Maybe this town won't be here anymore?" a farm worker in the article speculates.

By summer 2014, drought covered 100 percent of California, with 76 percent of the state experiencing extreme drought conditions. These are remarkable and terrifying circumstances, certain to lead to forest fires and agricultural devastation. But it is hard to look at a drought as an emergency — it quickly becomes the new normal. A farm worker in the *LA Times* article comments that, "Drought is different from other natural disasters because it doesn't end." My boyfriend laughed when we saw a sign on the 101 freeway reading, "SERIOUS DROUGHT. DON'T WASTE WATER." "I thought it said 'serious thought,'" he said. Well, I reminded him, it *is* a serious thought.

In May, it took me two buses and almost two hours to get to Boyle Heights, the East Los Angeles neighborhood where Evergreen Memorial Park and Crematory is nestled. Evergreen, established in 1877, is the oldest graveyard in Los Angeles and one of the largest, housing 300,000 graves in its 67 acres. Evergreen is a fascinating cemetery. Its "Garden of the Pines" is a monument to Japanese pioneers, and rows of beautiful Japanese graves lace through the rest of the park like veins.

Evergreen is different than other Los Angeles cemeteries — it feels less preened, more chaotic. Its grass grows sometimes green, sometimes yellow, straggling in dehydrated patches or failing altogether, revealing expanses of bare dirt. Amid the Japanese graves are monuments to LA's early movers and shakers, or as Ehrenreich puts it in "The End," a "stratum of dead whites with streets named after them." This includes John Edward Hollenbeck, who sold the city the land that would be Exposition Park, and Theodore Rimpau, whose massive Rancho Las Cienegas became much of West Los Angeles. Isaac Lankershim and Isaac Newton Van Nuys are also buried there, Otis's important collaborators in the Los Angeles Suburban Homes Company and the scheme to develop the San Fernando Valley. There are layers of irony here — the graves of men who went to great lengths to keep Los Angeles evergreen grow up amid yellow grass in a cemetery called Evergreen. When I was there, I saw a family gathered around a grave, watering it with a hose.

Evergreen illustrates why its men with streets named after them had to dream up Los Angeles so completely, lending it the same artificiality that Waugh disdained in Forest Lawn. Los Angeles is not a city that could ever have existed naturally — given its natural resources — in its current form. In "Half in Love with Easeful Death," Waugh makes a confident prediction about the end of Los Angeles. "It will be destroyed by drought," he writes.

> Its water comes 250 miles from the Colorado River. A handful of parachutists or partisans anywhere along that vital aqueduct can make the coastal strip uninhabitable. Bones will whiten along the Santa Fe trail as the great recession struggles Eastwards. Nature will re-assert herself and the seasons gently obliterate the vast, deserted suburb.

It was obvious to him that Los Angeles's hyper-development was no match for indifferent nature.

Los Angeles has several of the largest cemeteries in the world, emblems of the city's excessive nature, its belief in relationships of space and growth that only exist in the physics of dreams. But they also embody Los Angeles's relationship with destruction. Engineered to be a tropical paradise, a verdant ocean city enjoying everlasting youth, its citizens carry on in spite of the imminence of many natural emergencies, including droughts, fires, mudslides, and earthquakes. Its giant cemeteries are both an attempt to control death and evidence of the city's strange comfort with it. Didion writes in her essay "Los Angeles Days" about the "apparent equanimity" with which Los Angeles residents meet disaster, the fragility of the dream. "Something in the human spirit," she writes, "rejects planning on a daily basis for catastrophe." On the plaque in Hollywood Forever, the *Los Angeles Times* finally wishes farewell to its "martyred men" with this Los Angeles signature denial. "Forever green be the turf which California," it reads, "through all her perennial summertime, will graciously tend above their cherished graves!"

PLACING OF CONCRETE IN A SECTION OF THE COUNTERFORTED CHANNEL WALL ON THE LEFT BANK JUST ABOVE 26TH STREET IN THE CITY OF LOS ANGELES, 1938. US NATIONAL ARCHIVES AND RECORDS ADMINISTRATION.

ARTIST PORTFOLIO

HENRY TAYLOR

Everywhere in Henry Taylor's paintings, walls. There is hardly a painting of Taylor's that does not have a wall in it, somewhere, in many instances obscuring — or constituting — the horizon. No big skies here. Jesse Owens hurtles around a running track, but behind him, where one would expect banks of cheering crowds, a high white wall rises abruptly. A couple lounge on their couch, but through the window behind them, writing on a long prison wall advises inmates: "WARNING SHOTS NOT REQUIRED." The dome of the United States Capitol is glimpsed peeking above a white wall. Even the Amazonian figure of a woman in a white swimsuit — an icon of proud, liberated self-possession — is fenced in by a distant wall on which a notice about lifeguards seems like another kind of warning.

Freedom and its opposite fight it out in Taylor's paintings. Perhaps that is why Taylor paints like he does: fast, without premeditation, sticking to no rules, not overthinking his pictures. If the paint drips, it drips. As a painter he remains light on his feet, responsive to the world. He paints whoever is in front of him, or invites neighbors off the street to sit in his home or his Chinatown studio. He worked, years ago, as a psychiatric nurse in a state mental hospital and did portraits of the patients in his care there, when they would let him.

Taylor paints the people in his life, whether the daughter of his friend the artist Simone Leigh, or the artist Andrea Bowers, with whom he studied at CalArts. (It is a common misconception, examined in a new monograph on the artist published this fall by MoMA PS1, that Taylor is self-taught; in fact, he came to art education late in life, in his 30s.)

Many subjects come to Taylor through history, via an embedded folk mythology populated with athletes, musicians, and people made famous by newspaper stories. Carl Lewis, winning gold in the 1984 Olympic long jump, is pictured by Taylor leaping away from the high walls of a prison and over the white picket fence of a suburban home. *Another Wrong* (2013) shows a white man being led down a red path out of a Southern-style plantation home. The painting is based on an incident, immortalized by Bob Dylan in his song "The Lonesome Death of Hattie Carroll," which took place in Baltimore in 1963. A drunken young farmer named William Zantzinger had assaulted a black barmaid, who died from her injuries; he received a fine and six months in county jail for her manslaughter. In county, he never had to share cells with the overwhelmingly black inmates of the federal prison.

"This is America and if you're black in America it's easy for politics to permeate your work," Taylor has said. That is to say, he does not set out to make political art, but as with other figure painters like Leon Golub or Alice Neel or Sylvia Sleigh — all of whom might be considered his artistic kin — once the door to individual human experience is opened, politics soon rush in behind. Taylor is finding a way, like these other artists, to make history paintings that reflect a history he feels a part of.

—JONATHAN GRIFFIN

SEE ALICE JUMP, 2011
ACRYLIC ON CANVAS
76 1/2" X 113"

ALL IMAGES, UNLESS OTHERWISE NOTED, ARE COURTESY OF THE ARTIST AND BLUM & POE, LOS ANGELES

SWEET, 2012
ACRYLIC ON CANVAS
75" X 96" X 2 1/2"

TENNESSEE REBEL, 2009
ACRYLIC ON CANVAS
52" X 48"
COURTESY OF THE ARTIST AND UNTITLED, NEW YORK

THE LONG JUMP BY CARL LEWIS, 2010
ACRYLIC ON CANVAS
87.5" X 77"
COURTESY OF THE ARTIST AND UNTITLED, NEW YORK

"WATCH YOUR BACK," 2013
ACRYLIC ON CANVAS
87 1/2" X 77 1 / 2" X 2"

ANDREA BOWERS, 2010
ACRYLIC ON CANVAS
28" X 24"
COURTESY OF THE ARTIST AND UNTITLED, NEW YORK

NOAH, 2011
ACRYLIC ON CANVAS
96 1/2" X 76 3/4"

JESSE OWENS IN '36, 2010
ACRYLIC ON CANVAS
87.5" X 77"
COURTESY OF THE ARTIST AND UNTITLED, NEW YORK

SIMONE LEIGH'S DAUGHTER ZENOBIA, 2014
ACRYLIC ON CANVAS
70" X 58 3/4"

MARY HAD A LITTLE . . . (THAT AIN'T NO LAMB), 2013
ACRYLIC ON CANVAS
96 1/2" X 71 3/4" X 2 1/2"

ANOTHER WRONG, 2013
ACRYLIC ON CANVAS
116" X 75 1/2" X 2 1/2"

"SPLIT," 2013
ACRYLIC AND CHARCOAL ON CANVAS; TWO PARTS; 72" X 60" X 2 1/2" EACH

MARVIN
GAYE

RESTING, 2011
ACRYLIC AND COLLAGE ON CANVAS
64" X 77 3/4"

THAT'S MY BABY SISTER, 2011
ACRYLIC ON CANVAS
93 1/2" X 77"

"OF THE MAKING OF MANY BOOKS THERE IS NO END"

REMEMBERING MICHAEL KAMMEN, THE PROFESSOR OF PARADOX

DOUGLAS GREENBERG

My mentor and friend Michael Kammen died last November. A widely published and Pulitzer Prize–winning author, his passing was duly noted in *The New York Times*, *The Washington Post*, and other newspapers. The newsletters of various historical organizations also printed warm and admiring obituaries.

Individually some of these death notices contained factual errors or interpretive eccentricities that Michael would have found amusing, although he was too meticulous a scholar to have committed such mistakes himself. Collectively, however, they described a scholar and university professor who was literally prodigious.

He was a dedicated citizen of his country and his profession, serving on a dozen nonprofit boards from the New York State Historical Association to the Smithsonian. He was elected to the Council of the American Historical Association and as President of the Organization of American Historians. His CV, including all his publications, runs 35 closely spaced pages. Listed on paper, his achievements seem so vast that they could easily have made for three or four distinguished careers rather than one.

Michael's final book, *Digging Up the Dead*, was published three years earlier: a darkly humorous work on the morbid 19th-century American habit of disinterring famous Americans and reburying them. It was, in some ways, the sort of book a scholar might write in mid-career, having proven himself or herself capable of deep and serious research but seeking to track a new course of scholarship. In Michael's case, as we shall see, it was no such thing since he had been publishing surprising books on unpredictable subjects since his 30s. It was a coda, not a transition.

After *Digging Up the Dead* was published, Michael was progressively overtaken by a series of health problems (mainly debilitating pain in his back and neck). It became impossible for him to continue to do what he had done his whole life: devote every available hour not just to digging up the dead, but to communing with them, spending his days immersed in his sources, writing and teaching about what he discovered.

It was then, when he was no longer physically capable of the sustained concentration that a new book would demand, that he turned to the *Los Angeles Review of Books* as a venue for shorter pieces. But a short essay by Michael Kammen was, even when he was so ill, the sort of thing that any writer would have been proud to produce. First, there was the lustrous prose. Then there were the subjects, which ranged from essays about Gore Vidal, Howard Zinn, and Jack Kerouac to one about Leonardo and Michelangelo, to meditations on various aspects of American art — the passion that had absorbed so much of his attention in the previous 20 years or so. There were nine of these essays published in *LARB* in 2012 and 2013; the last, a contemplation of the origins of the movie industry, appeared only three weeks before his death. It contained, as did almost everything Michael wrote, a statement of irony, contradiction, and paradox to characterize his subject, which he said expressed both "rampant capitalist greed and the transformation of visual experience."

These essays for *LARB*, on an amazingly diverse set of subjects, were deeply satisfying to a man who needed to write the way the rest of us need to breathe, but he also wished he had the stamina to return to book-writing. He wrote to tell me about his essay in *LARB* on political cartoons, "Poking Serious Fun by Making Frivolous Art," in July of 2013: "This seems to be what I do these days — my day job, as it were." Indeed, a scan of the titles of both his books and these final articles leaves the same impression: how could one person contain within his intellectual life so broad a range of interests and concerns and write so brilliantly about all of them? Michael Kammen wrote or edited 32 books. He authored more than 165 essays in scholarly and professional journals and hundreds of book reviews. He also spoke widely around the country and the world, delivering 240 invited lectures over the course of a 45-year career spent exclusively at Cornell University. He won 10 major fellowships and an equal number of major national prizes and awards. He taught thousands of Cornell undergraduates and was a demanding but always popular teacher. He also supervised a couple dozen doctoral dissertations, chaired his department, and served his university in several administrative posts.

Because he closed his career with these fascinating essays in the *Los Angeles Review of Books*, this seems an appropriate venue for a reminiscence of his work and his life as the first anniversary of his death approaches.

Michael began his career as a standard-issue scholar-teacher, with a Harvard PhD under the supervision of the great historian of early American history, Bernard Bailyn. When he appeared in Cambridge for the first time in the autumn of 1958 he had already written a book, entitled *Operational History of the Flying Boat*. While it was a book Michael silently dropped from his CV in later years, it lived on as an enduring amusement to his graduate students.

Kammen's work under Bailyn coincided with the presence in Bailyn's seminars of a truly unusual cohort of fellow graduate students, many of whom went on to become noted historians themselves. In addition to Michael, there were, in a brief span of years, Stanley Katz, Gordon Wood, James Henretta, Richard Bushman, Richard Buel, Pauline Maier, and Philip Greven, along with many others. Bailyn was then interested in the politics of the British Empire, and Kammen, Katz, and Henretta each wrote doctoral dissertations that became books on various aspects of the subject.

Truth be told, while important, the politics of the British Empire did not exactly make for thrilling prose, and none of the three built scholarly careers by pursuing the subject. After making their bones on imperial politics, they all moved on to other things just as Bailyn himself would do. One reviewer of Michael's contribution, *A Rope of Sand: The Colonial Agents, British Politics, and the American Revolution*, described the book as being "in the best tradition of post-Namierite indigestibility [for Lewis Namier, the renowned British historian of the subject]." That description was only partially deserved, but it was the last time Michael's prose would be criticized so harshly in print.

Michael had moved to Cornell University in Ithaca, New York, by then; it was a place he loved from the beginning, despite many tempting opportunities to move to other universities. Except for a few visiting posts at other institutions, it was the place where he remained for the rest of his life. In this age of superstar professors who become the academic equivalent of free agents in professional sports, it may seem a bit incongruous that a scholar as renowned as Michael Kammen not only chose to reject the offers of other institutions but also did not use them as bargaining chips for more money and less teaching at his home institution, a common strategy at the higher levels of academe.

Michael fell in love with Cornell undergraduates and, unsurprisingly, the history of Cornell as well. He enjoyed the company of his predecessor in early American History, Curtis P. Nettels, whose obituary he would write in 1981, and he was soon in the thrall of Carl L. Becker, the eminent historian who had epitomized the Cornell tradition in an earlier generation. Becker, who died in 1945, wrote a book about the early history of the university, the central theme of which was the dyad and frequent paradox of freedom and responsibility. Becker was wide-ranging in precisely the way Michael would be: he wrote a doctoral dissertation on the American Revolution that shaped scholarly debate for most of the 20th century, and authored several books of sublime essays on problems of historical writing and thinking, as well as on the Enlightenment and the French Revolution.

Michael was taken with Becker as a historical thinker, referred to him often throughout his career, and would soon edit Becker's letters — which can still be read for their wisdom on everything from the travails of graduate education to the relationship between history and politics. I served as Michael's research assistant on the Becker volume entitled *What Is the Good of History?*, echoing a question Becker had posed in a letter. (When the book was complete and I was about to leave Cornell for my own first academic job, Michael gave me a copy with the following inscription: "For Doug, Who after four years in Ithaca, may still be asking the question that gives this book its name.") When Michael died, his wife Carol buried him in an Ithaca cemetery next to Carl Becker so the two could be together in death, as they were in life.

Early on in his career, Michael taught according to the style of his own training: as a "colonial historian," a characterization that soon would become a vexed and deservedly criticized way to describe scholarship in a field whose chief concerns were still mainly about white men in Virginia and Massachusetts. His view was more nuanced, but he was already headed in another direction. He wrote four more books in early American history and edited three others. Then he wrote the book that both culminated his career in early American scholarship and launched him on the next phase of his journey: *People of Paradox: An Inquiry Concerning the Origins of American Civilization*.

Published when he was only 36, *People* (as his graduate students called it) was an audacious book for a young man to write in a field replete with authoritative senior figures (including his mentor, Bailyn). It proposed not only to reinterpret the whole of American history to 1789, but also suggested that patterns set in those years determined the shape of the subsequent history of the United States. In addition, the prose was not conventionally academic: not only was it readable, it was lush and rhythmic and beautiful. *People* was also a book on the subject of historical "syzygies" that had a "Prolegomenon" and an "Epilogism." The book was innovative in substance and in composition. And it was pathbreaking in other ways too, peppered with images, most not well known, illustrating Michael's argument that the American past was a mélange of contradiction on matters ranging from politics and economics to social structure and race, and that these paradoxes were the explanatory apparatus for everything else that American culture encompassed.

Michael intended *People* as a cultural history (a field that had not quite been invented yet) that would reach not only into high culture for evidence but also into popular culture. The genuinely paradoxical relationship between the two in the 17th and 18th centuries was sufficiently compelling that Michael would later write a book about their interconnection in the 20th century. By the time *People* was published in 1972, he had written or edited close to a dozen books in early American history and was regarded as one of the young leaders of the field, which he promptly abandoned — permanently, as it turned out — to explore other aspects of American history.

People of Paradox made Michael Kammen about as famous as any academic historian could be. Winning the Pulitzer created many opportunities for him to travel and lecture in this country and overseas, which he did frequently and happily for the rest of his life. As late as a year ago, he went to Argentina to give lectures, despite being in dire and constant pain. Travel was, for Michael, another opportunity to learn. He was insatiably curious; his trips were invariably followed by fascinating travelogues filled with telling descriptions of those he had met and what he had seen.

He also collected postcards and little slips of hotel stationery wherever he went. These would then become the media for communicating with friends and students after he returned. A postcard with an Ithaca postmark would appear in my mailbox, but the postcard itself would show me a temple in Kyoto or a sculpture in Delhi or a restaurant in Paris. Soon a thick envelope would arrive from Ithaca with photos, newspaper clippings, and bibliographic suggestions, but the cover note, written in Michael's precise hand, appeared on stationery from a hotel in London or Geneva or Tehran.

These postcards and envelopes, which all his friends and students received regularly, were the core of Michael's character. He was interested in everything, and he was not only consumed by his own omnivorous curiosity — he carried the curiosities of others along with him on his travels. He had a prescient capacity to find facts, books, articles, pictures, artifacts, and people who would answer or, better, raise questions in which others would be interested. When email came along, we all continued to hear from our friend regularly, but we missed the postcards and exotic hotel stationery.

A scholar of such formidable achievements might have been intimidating to students and colleagues, but Michael Kammen was anything but. His curiosity and enthusiasm were almost childlike. When he asked you a question, he asked because he was unpretentiously interested in the answer, not because he was quizzing you or trying to show you up. As an insecure first-year grad student, I once nervously laughed when Michael mentioned that the author of a book we had read had died of a brain tumor. Mine was an infantile reaction driven by anxiety. Almost anyone else would have thought that he had a pretty awful person sitting at his seminar table, but Michael merely asked me with complete sincerity why I was laughing. He simply assumed that I must have had a good reason to laugh, a reason he didn't understand, and he wanted to know what it was. That's the way he was about everything: he assumed that if you said or did something there was a good reason, however inappropriate or ignorant it might have appeared to anyone else. In fact, years later I reminded him of my outburst in his seminar, saying I had felt terribly about it. With complete and uncomplicated good will, he said: "I remember that, but I never quite understood what you were laughing at. I've never been able to figure it out."

He was also, sometimes inexplicably, uncompetitive with his peers. Certain scholars spend more time watching what others are doing and disparaging it than doing their own work. Professional envy among scholars is, the joke goes, so intense because the stakes are so low. But Michael did not feel diminished by other people's accomplishments, and he was truly befuddled when he observed their *schadenfreude*. When others succeeded, Michael was always supportive and happy for them. In all our years of friendship, I hardly ever heard him utter a negative word about another person. His professional judgments embodied high standards, but they sought the best in others. On the two or three occasions when he told me that something he said or did prompted hostility from others, he expressed regret that he had not handled the situation more adroitly. He was kind by nature. "A simply lovely man," was how Carol described him after he died.

His curiosity and his generosity of spirit were not only his characteristic way of being in the world. They also explain both the quality and quantity of his writing. His curiosity drove him always to keep reading, researching, and writing; his generosity prevented him from being distracted by professional rivalry and one-upmanship. He loved the story of the Duke of Gloucester who, upon receiving a volume of Edward Gibbon's still incomplete *The Decline and Fall of the Roman Empire*, said, "Another damned thick book! Always scribble, scribble, scribble! Eh, Mr. Gibbon?" That was, of course, Michael too: he was always scribbling and, like Gibbon, to great good effect.

In the middle of his career, Michael completed a trilogy that was arguably his most enduring contribution to modern historical scholarship. He shifted from writing about history itself to what a more theoretically minded scholar would have called meta-history: the history of how people recall their own past. Prompted to this inquiry by Becker's presidential address to the American Historical Association in 1931, "Everyman His Own Historian," Michael began with the American Revolution in *A Season of Youth: The American Revolution and the Historical Imagination*. Then he turned to the Constitution in *A Machine that Would Go of Itself: The Constitution in American Culture*. Finally he wrote what is arguably his true magnum opus: *Mystic Chords of Memory: The Transformation of Tradition in American Culture*. In the same period of about a dozen years, he published three books of essays and edited two other volumes. Scribble, scribble, scribble. Eh, Mr. Kammen?

Michael's memory project was a mammoth undertaking because it required him to do two very difficult things: acquire intellectual control of the historiography of the underlying subject and also master the place of that subject in the history of American culture. When he described what he was trying to do in conversation, it sounded simple — but it wasn't. The research effort for this project was truly massive, just as the analysis it inspired required a more subtle mind than most historians possess. Each book was longer than the one before — *Mystic Chords* ran to almost 900 pages, prompting me to tease him that I thought he must never have met a note card (now an archaic technology) he didn't like. These books also exemplify other traits of Michael's that were apparent throughout his life: his eye for the revealing but unremembered image and his ear for the telling but usually overlooked quotation.

The memory trilogy expanded Michael's audience to include scholars in other fields of history and in other disciplines as well, because the really big problem with which he was trying to grapple, the relationship between history and memory, was one that had real traction in other fields of knowledge and profound meaning in other cultures. As had happened with early American history, however, just as Michael's work was beginning to receive broad recognition for its unique contribution, he moved on to other things.

It would be a mistake to see Michael Kammen only as a relentlessly driven scholar, although he was surely that. He found time for many other pleasures: Carol and his sons and eventual daughters-in-law and grandchildren were at the top of that list. His notes and emails to me were filled with news of his family and the happiness they brought him. He also appreciated fine wine and food, an offshoot of his many travels. No professional meeting was complete without a restaurant and a fine wine he'd selected himself. He was a man of sophisticated and cosmopolitan tastes, but he was also paradoxically protean in his interests. He was an avid fan of college and professional sports — and not in an especially academic way. Michael once good-naturedly described an obsequious graduate student with an encyclopedic knowledge of professional football, as a "jock sniffer." He watched the NFL and the NBA religiously, but his great love was college basketball. Once, years ago when I was teaching at Princeton, he came to deliver a lecture, which was followed by a cocktail party in our home for the assembled Princeton worthies, many of them historians Michael admired. But it was the Monday night of the end of March Madness and, as game time approached, Michael pulled me aside to suggest we ask everyone to leave since we simply *had* to see The Game from opening tip to final basket. With great conspiratorial amusement, we ushered some of the best historians in the country out the door.

Sports were one of the things about which Michael and I disagreed. There were some other less important subjects (like books and music and art) where our opinions occasionally diverged, but our disagreement about basketball and baseball was fundamental. First, Michael was one of only a very few historians I know who did not think baseball in every way a pastime superior to all others. He was a basketball guy. Second, and almost unforgivably, he hated the Yankees and had a suspiciously atavistic affection for the Red Sox. Since love of baseball and the Yankees were about as close as I could come to religious beliefs, I played along with him about college basketball and he humored me about baseball.

We did share an affection for using baseball metaphors to describe professional experiences, however. When the superb American historian John Higham visited Cornell to give a series of lectures named for Carl Becker, Michael wrote me that he had introduced Higham by saying that if American historians were a baseball team, Higham would be the center fielder. We made a game of deciding in which positions we would play other historians on our metaphorical team. On another occasion, I chaired a session at a meeting of historians in which Michael, his mentor Bud Bailyn, and our mutual hero, John Hope Franklin, gave papers. Michael knew I wasn't joking when I introduced the session by saying I felt like a utility infielder from the minor leagues playing catch with Lou Gehrig, Babe Ruth, and Jackie Robinson.

No message from Michael was complete without a reference to what he was reading, and it became a sort of ritual with us to exchange reading recommendations but rarely about narrowly professional books. We tended to focus on contemporary literary fiction and nonfiction. Once or twice we found ourselves reading the same book at the same time. Books of all kinds — writing them and reading them — were everything to Michael. It was always a privilege to have him as a sounding board on what I was reading and to know that he wanted to share the pleasures of his own reading with me. When Philip Roth's *The Plot Against America* came out, Michael (who had sometimes teased me about my New Jersey roots) wrote: "Do you recommend the new Roth? I realize that you are from the neighborhood, but is it in the same league with HUMAN STAIN and AMERICAN PASTORAL, both of which I thought were excellent, esp. the former." I did recommend it, although I allowed that I didn't think it quite up to the standard of the other two Roth volumes.

And Michael kept scribbling. After finishing the memory trilogy, he made a turn that I am told surprised some people, but which his friends expected. He began to write about American art, as well as about American culture. He was a collector, even a connoisseur, of American art. In the late '80s, I was Vice President of the American Council of Learned Societies in New York. (Michael's grad-school friend Stanley Katz was the President.) Michael occasionally asked me to pick up something he had purchased from a New York dealer and hold on to it until he could make the trip from Ithaca to get it. I especially remember his retrieving an item that seemed to have special importance to him and regaling my colleagues with a vivid description of what I had looked like when I was 20 pounds lighter and my hair 10 inches longer.

But the new work in art history could have been foretold even from Michael's earliest scholarship. He always had an eye for images, and all his books included them, even the "indigestible" *Rope of Sand*. The use of images is a more common practice among historians now than it was then. At the time, neither the historians nor the art historians knew what to make of Michael. For him, artistic expression and history were inextricably connected to one another; anything a culture produced represented a pathway to understanding its history and its understanding of itself. As a result, he continued to write about culture generally even as he turned to art.

In 1999, he published two books: *American Culture, American Tastes: Social Change and the 20th Century* and *Robert Gwathmey: The Life and Art of a Passionate Observer*. The former ranged widely across the 20th century and echoed, both in method and in substance, the insights he had first developed in *People of Paradox* about high, low, and, he now added, middlebrow culture. The latter was, he later told me, his favorite of all his books: a biography of the social realist painter, Robert Gwathmey, it is a simply beautiful book — to hold, to look at, and to read. Michael loved that project so much that he said he was sorry to finish it. And he also took enormous pleasure in the Gwathmey pieces he was able to add to his collection and in his friendship with Gwathmey's architect son, Charles.

Michael Kammen loved a good joke, and not a few bad ones. His laugh was not a giggle but a guffaw. The internet, when it arrived, offered him the opportunity to indulge his affection for the comic arts, as well as to tell the same terrible joke to 20 friends simultaneously. Michael's emailed jokes actually got to be a joke themselves among his friends, because it was so "un-Michael" to see a silly and sometimes vulgar internet joke appear under his name when all of us thought him a person of fine and penetrating sensibilities. I once mentioned this to him, and he said: "It's a paradox."

His students joked that we were members of the Kammenwealth — but all we had in common was our love for Michael, our professor of paradox. We had not come to Cornell to study a subject; we had come to work with him. And those were personal, not only academic, aspirations.

A close reading of his work really does reveal that paradox, contradiction, and irony were the leitmotif of everything he wrote. No historian of his generation published as much high-quality scholarship as Michael, yet he was strangely without influence on the larger field of American history because his interests were so unique that no one knew quite where to place him in American historiography. There was no school of interpretation or method associated with Michael. His books evoked admiring but frequently bemused reviews because no one else knew enough about his subjects to be very critical.

Over many years, really going back to his earliest writings in the 1960s and 1970s, Michael was fascinated by the lives of historians and the relationship between personal experience and scholarly work. His was not a simplistic rendering of these relationships either; he approached them with great subtlety and sensitivity, aiming to understand and locate historical thinking in both culture and lived experience. The number of historians — mostly but not only Americanists — whose work he considered in print is extremely large. He was trying to read their work and correspondence in the context of the long history of the entire discipline, and he attempted to understand what drove them to do the kind of work they did. This part of Michael's corpus is too little read and appreciated. It was not a once-over-lightly project either, but the product of more of his uniquely original research.

When Michael visited libraries and archives, as he so often did when working on his major book projects, he always set aside some time to examine the papers of any historian who might have left correspondence in the depository he was visiting. Over the years, the list of scholars whose private papers Michael had read grew quite long. For the most part, he was dissatisfied with historians' published and usually guarded autobiographies because he sought a deeper, more intimate understanding of what drove historical scholarship. The result of all this research and thought was a string of essays, some about individual historians and some on more general questions of historiography.

The best of these, I thought, was "Personal Identity and the Historian's Vocation," the lead essay in Michael's collection *In the Past Lane* (1997). It began: "Perhaps I personify a curious paradox." This one was the historian's goal of detachment (which was eloquently described by Michael's hero, Carl Becker) versus the undoubted fact that historians, like others, are driven by internal forces arising from personal background and values. The essay is a wonderful introduction to Michael's thinking, characterized by remarkably deep research in the papers of many historians.

"Personal Identity and the Historian's Vocation" also revealed implicitly how influenced Michael had been by the social forces that swirled around his own professional life. The essay contained long sections on historians whose work had been self-consciously shaped by aspects of personal identity: race, class, gender, and sexual orientation. As was his custom, he couldn't simply write a few platitudinous lines to show that he was politically correct. Instead, he dug deeply into the work and personal lives of such scholars as the peerless John Hope Franklin, David Montgomery, Fawn Brodie, and John D'Emilio. All of this was in service of understanding the paradox of the historical profession's commitment to detachment, which, in the end, Michael concluded was not only impossible, but undesirable.

Interested as he was in the papers of other historians, he left surprisingly little himself when he died. He had once commented that "I do not for a minute deny that some historians have been exceedingly private — seemingly programmed — like Charles and Mary Beard, to destroy their papers so that subsequent snoops like myself would not be able to make such connections [between the personal and the professional]." He was, in other words, utterly fascinated by the papers of others and exploited them brilliantly as a historiographer, but he was fairly ruthless in doing what the Beards had done, destroying his own papers in characteristically systematic fashion.

When I discovered how little he had retained of his own correspondence after his death, I was surprised and disappointed. He was the most meticulous and well-organized person I have ever known, and I knew that he had corresponded with all his contemporaries as part of his historiographic project. I also knew he had what Stan Katz calls a "Google-like filing system before Google." His interest in other historians was insatiable, as his many essays, obituaries, and thematic essays on other scholars demonstrated. Candidly, I had hoped to get a peek at some of his own files because I am precisely the same kind of "snoop" he was. But he was also, as I had known, a very private person who did not talk very much about his own background or psychology. We knew each other for decades, but I don't think we ever had more than a cursory conversation about the intensely Jewish background we shared or about the many differences and similarities between us that we both recognized and appreciated. Michael preserved the past of other historians but discarded most of the unpublished record of his own career.

Although he was interested in the lives of others, Michael was in life a reserved and self-contained man, and he remained so in death. He lived many of his hours and days in the past, visiting the dead, and he reported voluminously on what he learned from them, but he spent little time or energy on his own past, even his professional past. He was relentless about focusing on his next project. When he died, his library study at Cornell did not have any of his own books in it and no notes from previous research. It was filled instead with all sorts of books from every part of the library, which Carol described to me:

> On the shelf there were books about the Bennington Monuments, the New Jersey Tercentenary, the *Intimate History of Humanity* by Theodore Zeldin, whom we both revere, and Goldwin Smith's *Reminiscences*. There was John Franklin Jameson's book on humanistic scholarship and a book on the transitional turn in American Studies, something that bothered him. There was a book called the *States of Memory*, and another on the *Collective Memory of Political Events*. There was a book he had brought home and read, then returned to the study entitled *The Newspaper in Art*, and there was Richard Shiff's *Doubt*.

There were also notes he had taken on various books and sources to which he would want to return or about which he wanted to write. He saved relatively few letters, either from him or to him (he culled them regularly over the years along with his library), although he was paradoxically a faithful and insightful correspondent.

For a younger generation of historians, I fear Kammen's work may seem old-fashioned, uninformed as it is by theory and, with the exception of the Gwathmey book, not narrowly focused upon race, class, and gender. Paradoxically, however, a close reading of Michael's entire body of work — not only his meditations on historiography — will reveal that he was too conscious of his nation's record of contradiction and hypocrisy not to have been alive to the significance of race, class, and gender in its history. His big project of elucidating American culture rarely left race, class, and gender out of the equation. And he had thought about, researched, and seriously considered writing about gay men in American culture. He never published anything on the subject because he didn't feel confident that he understood the complexity of the history well enough to do a good job. More paradoxes.

Late in the spring of 2006, in the course of a long email about something else, Michael wrote:

> Did I tell you that an MRI showed that I have osteo-arthritis, mainly in the cervical (neck) part of my vertebrae. The disks & cartilage separating the v's have worn thin, and I have a pinched nerve. Tingling in my right neck and shoulder side. I go 3x per week for physical therapy and do 5 exercises at home. Traction to pull the v's apart. Plus a special heat pad on my neck 3 or 4x per day. Now I need to write for a buckwheat pillow! Known to help. I can still go to the YMCA for exercise and ride my bike. Like Roth's new novel, all about aging!

At the time, I worried a bit about how painful this must have been, but Michael was nearing 70, and I chalked it up to his both sitting at his desk all day and being a six-times-per-week gym rat and runner. He was as meticulous about his health as he was about other things. I admired and failed to emulate his discipline about exercise.

Unfortunately, this was the beginning of a long decline in his health, which I think he found torturous, not only because it was painful, but also because it got in the way of his work. Still, the emails kept coming; a few weeks later he wrote to report how thrilled he was that Cornell had finally named a dorm for Carl Becker. But the pain was persistent. In an email mainly about a documentary film on which he wanted my opinion, his new grandson, and the new junior history faculty at Cornell, he wrote: "I'm not sure that the phys. therapy is making much of a difference. Still dealing with a pain in the neck, though it moves back and forth between my shoulder and my neck. Tomorrow I get a home traction kit. Fun!"

The slowness of his rehabilitation was now a presence in all his mails. Yet he kept working, writing a long essay on the history of American photography and writing new lectures for his course on the history of American culture (which he had been teaching brilliantly for 30 years or so). Yet another new book also appeared that summer, *Visual Shock: A History of Art Controversies in American Culture*, and he wrote of it, as he frequently did of his books, as though it were one of his children: "The project really was a labor of love, and I miss it now that it is totally out of my hands and house."

About a year later, he mentioned for the first time that he was planning to retire at the end of 2008. Characteristically, he also offhandedly mentioned that he was going to give a Jefferson Lecture at Berkeley, where his son, Daniel, was (and is) one of the leading energy scientists in the United States. The note was more about Daniel's accomplishments than Michael's. But a conference I had helped organize honoring his old friend, Stan Katz, had set him to thinking in a more introspective way. He worried that a great fuss would be made about his retirement and said he really hoped I wouldn't take part in organizing such a thing for him because it would make him uncomfortable. In fact, I had begun to think about what might be done to celebrate his career at Cornell and in the world beyond, but I took him at his word: we organized something small in Ithaca, which, in the end, I could not attend because of the weather there in midwinter.

But he was thinking hard about these things:

> I also don't have a major project in the works — 1st time in 45 years. So one has a sense of transition, not so much a life complete as a career nearing completion. "Retirement" is a very strange thing to contemplate. It's a concept that always applied to others, not yourself. Even though I sort of keep busy (writing a lot of book reviews, eg), I still have unaccustomed time on my hands. Life simply slows down, and one spends more time dealing with aches, pains, and illnesses of all sorts, and doctors and pharmacies. One does not feel the end is nigh. It might be, but actuarial tables say I could well have another 15 years. The question is, what to do with them beside read, go to the movies, read magazines, and plan travel (perhaps the Fjords this summer). If you have led a very busy life, it's a bit disconcerting trying to get used to being not so busy, and especially not busy with the vocation that you chose and always loved so much. It doesn't quite seem to matter very much any more.

These words were disturbing to me at the time, but I don't think I connected them directly to his neck and back pain. Still some distance from retirement myself, I figured this was the sort of stage-of-life thing that all retirees face. Perhaps it was.

But mortality and death, subjects we had never discussed, soon became a theme in our correspondence. A few days after that last message, he sent me one of his internet jokes, but it had a serious meaning for him:

> I want to live my next life backwards:
> You start out dead and get that out of the way.
> Then you wake up in an old age home feeling better every day.
> Then you get kicked out for being too healthy.
> You enjoy your retirement and collect your pension.
> Then when you start work, you get a gold watch on your first day.
> You work 40 years until you're too young to work.
> You get ready for High School: drink alcohol, party, and you're generally promiscuous.
> Then you go to primary school, you become a kid, you play, and you have no responsibilities.
> Then you become a baby, and then.....
> You spend your last 9 months floating peacefully in luxury, in spa-like conditions: central heating, room service on tap, and then,
> You finish off as an orgasm.

Michael and I kept in close touch during these years, but we didn't see each other often. I was living in Los Angeles, and he was in Ithaca. When he came to the West Coast, he usually went to Berkeley to see Daniel and his family, and I had work that kept me traveling a great deal so I stopped attending the professional meetings that had long been our opportunity for a dinner and long talk. Fortunately, he received an invitation to give a seminar at the Getty in the fall of 2007, and Michael and my wife, Margee, and I had a wonderful, though hurried, breakfast with him overlooking the Sepulveda Pass. We did comment to each other that he seemed to have slowed down a bit, but since he had been in motion as long as we had known him, reducing his speed from 100 miles an hour to 75 didn't seem a bad thing.

Then his retirement was suddenly upon me. I wrote him at length about it, saying among other things that I thought studying with him when I was a young man, apart from marrying Margee, was either the luckiest or the smartest thing I had ever done. He wrote a beautiful note in return, in which he described the "low-key" departure celebration that his colleagues had organized, and he expressed relief that it wasn't anything more than that. Then — and this did not surprise me — he mentioned that he was about to begin work on another book after all, but wasn't certain what the topic would be, saying he had to make a choice between two subjects, one of which was the "American habit of digging up and reburying famous people." That became *Digging Up the Dead.* I later discovered that he also wrote the other book, but never published it.

Whatever malaise he had been expressing before his retirement seemed to lift a bit, and soon another email arrived telling me that his other son, Douglas (whose email from Michael I sometimes received by mistake), had taken a job as a political scientist at the National University of Singapore, and that Michael and Carol were soon to see Douglas and his family with a stop in Berkeley for time with Daniel and his wife and daughters. In addition, he was now sending me drafts of new essays for comment, something that had tailed off when he first told me about the pain he was suffering. There was a new energy, although he was writing in a more reflective way about his personal experiences as a historian, as a mentor of graduate students for example. He and Carol came to LA that spring, and the four of us had a great evening at Joe's in Venice before we dropped them at LAX to take a red-eye back to the East Coast. "If they can still take the red-eye," Margee said, "Michael must be feeling better." And he was traveling quite a lot as he had throughout his career: lectures in Turkey, Germany, Romania all coming in quick succession. All good news. Hardly a paradox in sight.

But Michael's health was in a steady decline; he surprised us with news that he had a quintuple bypass operation in August of 2008, and was frustrated that he had to cancel lectures in Utah and Paris. He recovered more slowly than the doctors promised, and that too frustrated him. We had moved to New Jersey by then, and he was well enough for a reunion dinner in New York the following winter where he also received the American Historical Association's Award for Scholarly Distinction. But he was in continuous physical therapy for his pain, and it wasn't helping very much. He wrote: "Actually, what I have is called spinal stenosis and neurogenic .... something I can't even spell. Lots of pills. MRI last Thursday. Reading images tomorrow." By early 2011, he was feeling well enough to fly to Hawaii for a family vacation with Daniel and Douglas and their families, but wrote me:

> Our trip to Maui was hard on my back, but worth it. The whole family hadn't been together for 4 years... Surgery has been postponed while they try a new drug for pain and medical patches on the bad areas. The herniated disk is on hold. So we'll see. But typing is just too hard on my back, so I'm doing almost none now. Reading a lot of books that I never got to...I'm not going to the OAH. Flying is just too tough.

Not being able to type was torture for Michael, but he could not resist making a joke of it at his own expense, noting the paradox of being a writer who couldn't use a keyboard. He was just as aggrieved by not being able to travel, something he loved to do — he was thrilled each time he received an invitation to lecture in a place he had never seen or one to which he was glad to return.

The battery of treatments did little to relieve Michael's ailments. The pace of our correspondence did not decline, however; if anything, it increased. And he began the wonderful series of pieces that he wrote for the *Los Angeles Review of Books* in this period. But he was in constant unendurable pain.

Finally, after every alternative had been exhausted, he underwent an extremely complicated and ultimately unsuccessful surgery in March of 2012. This left him on a ventilator for an unbearably long period of time, during which he could not speak, including three months on a feeding tube when he could not eat; he recovered from the ordeal, only to find the operation did little to alleviate his terrible pain. The emails about sports and books never paused, but they were foreshortened by his inability to sit before his computer for very long. I sent him the text of a commencement address I had been asked to give, filled with references to popular culture, recent and not so recent. He wrote me a nice note about it, which concluded:

> I've heard the name Jay-Z. No idea who Jackson Brown is. Fitzgerald didn't even need a first name, and Dylan is Dylan. Ever since I read POSITIVELY 4th STREET, I don't like him. Nice moral imperatives at the end, and agree that success doesn't guarantee happiness.

We finally found we could agree about baseball in one way: we both found the first half or so of Chad Harbach's *The Art of Fielding* to be utterly gorgeous and brilliant. We disagreed about the rest of the book.

Margee and I had not been to Ithaca in many years so we planned a trip at the end of October. We were anxious to see Michael and Carol, although it was clear from his emails that he was struggling still with the consequences of the surgery. We made the trip on the weekend before Hurricane Sandy hit, and the four of us had a wonderful time. Although hobbled and using a cane, Michael seemed himself in many ways, and even planned for us to go to a Cornell football game, an invitation we declined. It was just as well because it was obvious that he was in pain and the weather was forbidding (although Sandy left Ithaca pretty much unscathed). Nonetheless, there was something both thrilling and reassuring about the four of us being together again in Ithaca after a 45-year odyssey during which Margee and I had moved many times all over the country. Ithaca, and the company of Michael and Carol Kammen, felt like a safe harbor again.

Michael seemed to bounce back after that. The next spring he managed a trip to San Francisco for a meeting of the Organization of American Historians, which I could not attend. He organized his usual dinner for a group of former graduate students, but I was told later that he looked uncomfortable and stood for part of the meal. Michael never went anywhere without seeing whatever there was to see, so he took another of his former students out to Alcatraz and they spent an afternoon there, although it left him exhausted and in pain. When summer came, he and Carol went to Norway and then Michael went off to Buenos Aires to lecture for two weeks. Before he left he wrote me that he was going to fill a sudden vacancy at Cornell in the fall and teach an undergraduate seminar. He said he was as nervous about it as he had been when he arrived in 1965. I was also returning to teaching that fall after many years away, and we had an exchange about how old farts like us would deal with students whose attention span was limited to 140 characters at a time. But he was nervous about the trip to Argentina too. "I hope my back and neck are up to this. I've been taking life easy of late, and this will be fairly demanding." It was, and he returned exhausted, so much so that although he began to teach the scheduled course, he had to step away from it in late October.

There were a few more email exchanges about our experiences as "rookies" in the classroom and about the baseball playoffs, which were more important to me than the Jewish holidays and to him mostly an interruption of college football season. Margee and Carol stayed in touch too, but we knew that his health was precarious. He sent me a note on November 20 to say that a sentimental gift would soon arrive because "we now have more 'stuff' than we have space." A beautiful plate purchased in Japan on one of their trips there soon arrived, and we were touched.

On Friday evening, last November 29, Carol left us a voicemail telling us to call her as soon as we could. We were out very late that evening. I called the next morning. Carol told me that Michael had died the previous day, the day after Thanksgiving.

Losing Michael Kammen was as difficult as losing my parents. Stan Katz and I quickly wrote an obituary for the American Historical Association, and I chaired a session at the Organization of American Historians meeting last spring that was a collective tribute to Michael by his friends and students. I also accepted the invitation to write this tribute essay, although I could not bring myself to do it for some time.

Michael was an unusual and special man whose human and professional commitments seemed to be of a piece with one another. He was isolated up there in Ithaca. He liked to say, quoting Frances Perkins, that it was "the most centrally isolated spot on the Eastern Seaboard." I think he liked it that way, but he was also a wonderfully sociable person who went out of his way to befriend other scholars, especially those older and younger than he was. The professor of paradox was a sociable isolate. His friendship with John Higham, for example, connected him not only to Higham himself but also to Higham's mentor, Wisconsin's Merle Curti. His affection for Louis Masur, my Rutgers colleague and dear friend, connected him not only to me (years ago Lou's teacher) but also to Lou's student and Michael's young Cornell colleague, Aaron Sachs. Michael, even when he was sitting alone with his research and writing in his study in 710 Olin Library at Cornell in the middle of frozen Ithaca winter, was nonetheless also swimming in a warm and timeless sea of social connection that not only gave him great personal pleasure, but in which he was deeply interested as an academic matter. He was not only a sociable isolate, he was also a cerebral hedonist.

A distinguished scholar like Michael did not have to teach as much as he did, but he didn't approve of the impulse among many academics to regard teaching and scholarship as contradictory. When a very well-known historian, one of his Cornell colleagues, retired, he wrote me with rare sarcasm: "End of an era. ******** and his partner move to ****** in a week. He must be about 72. Has had life very cushy here for decades. Stopped teaching undergrads long ago." Michael, in contrast, relished teaching undergraduates. He thought Cornell students were wonderful, and he used his undergraduate courses to try out ideas that would eventually appear in his books and essays. New courses came along frequently, and different generations of Cornellians remember Michael as an expert on several dozen different aspects of American history as a result. Which, of course, he was.

He was a specialized generalist and a generalizing specialist, but the paradox of having both to teach and produce scholarship was one that Michael didn't understand. And that was a paradox too.

I don't know for certain, but I think people who didn't know Michael might have thought him obsessively careerist to have published so much for so long. He wasn't that at all, however; he *was* obsessed with his work but not by conventional standards of academic accomplishment. His obsession was curiosity. Our mutual friend, the brilliant historian Joyce Appleby, who has written about the history of curiosity, used to remind her students that everything they knew was the answer to a question someone else had asked. Michael had more curiosities and more questions than anyone I have ever known. His voluminous writing was his attempt to ask and to answer his questions with the rest of us watching and reading him as he went. Private curiosities pursued publicly.

And, miraculously, even when he could barely sit in front of his computer in his last years and when he told me he was through with writing books, the questions and curiosities and the need to pursue them in print continued. He had almost completed another book of essays, many previously unpublished. He planned yet another entitled "The Academic Life," and he wrote that series of charming pieces for *LARB*. His writing in those essays had a lightness and humor that was wonderful to behold. His lucid prose had always been unusually good for an academic; he was the most readable of serious historians and hated history that was "solid" but "dry" (his words). The *LARB* pieces were nothing but fun for him, and they were surprisingly playful as a result. My favorite was a review essay about Jack Kerouac, whom Michael described as a "Franco-American writer." I can see him smiling as he wrote that phrase.

"Jack Kerouac's Restless Odyssey and His New Life *On the Road*" was an appreciation of Kerouac through a review of a biography and a volume of Kerouac's letters. The highlight of the essay, however, was a personal story about Michael, who had invited Kerouac to visit Harvard when Michael was a senior tutor at Lowell House in 1964. Michael was anything but a hipster, and he must have been even less so in 1964. The visit went well in most ways, but Kerouac got very drunk and at two a.m. appeared in the courtyard of Lowell House and screamed (loud enough to wake Michael and Carol): "Fuck you, Mike Kammen." Paradoxically, that was surely the first and last time that anyone ever said "Fuck you" to him. It was also probably the only time anyone called him "Mike." He was neither a "Mike" nor a "fuck you" sort of guy.

I often reread my friend's books and essays. His authorial voice was so distinctive that they bring him back, as though he were sitting across the room or writing me a long email. They also stimulate my own interests and curiosities all over again, just as they did from the moment I met him in the fall of 1969. The personal and the professional, so often at odds in my own reading life, merge perfectly when I am reading Kammen. And that was another remarkable thing about him. As he said many times, he utterly loved being a historian, but he understood his profound professional identity as a sort of personal eccentricity that he never expected others to share. When my own career took some circuitous turns away from the life of the professor, Michael was never anything but the enthusiastic cheerleader. Even more, and especially in later years, he would tell me that my own work made a difference that the cloistered life of scholarship and teaching never could. I disagreed with that, of course, but I was always so grateful that, unlike so many graduate mentors, Michael did not expect me or any of his graduate students to live our lives in his image. He took pleasure in how much I had strayed from emulating him; he thought that it meant he had succeeded as my teacher. In this way too he echoed the career of the ever-present Carl Becker and another of his scholarly idols, the Stanford historian David Potter. Perhaps that is yet another paradox or two.

Years ago, when I went to retrieve that piece of art for him in New York, Michael told me that it was a watercolor by an artist he particularly liked, Leonard Baskin (born in my present home town of New Brunswick, New Jersey). At the time, I paid little attention. I appreciated his love of American art, but didn't quite share it. This past summer, Margee and I visited Carol, and saw the Baskin hanging on a wall in her house. I remembered it and its title: "Of the making of many books there is no end." It's a lovely watercolor of a scattered multicolor pile of books with the words of the painting's title in Hebrew below (a quote from Ecclesiastes). Carol and Daniel and Douglas thought I would like to have it and that Michael would want me to. It is now in my home, and I find myself staring at it daily, remembering my mentor, and friend.

"Of the making of many books there is no end." What better way to summarize Michael Kammen and his lifelong passion for books, for beauty, and for paradox. His making of many books did indeed have no end. He left two nearly complete manuscripts when he died and notes for others. Even in death, he is still making many books, both his own and those he inspires. But there's a paradox here too, one that gnaws at me.

The full quotation from Ecclesiastes is the following: "Of the making of many books there is no end; and much study is a weariness of the flesh." Michael was too careful a scholar not to have known the full quotation and its provenance before he purchased the painting. He would have been in his mid-50s when he bought it and asked me to pick it up for him. What was he thinking about the painting's meaning and significance in his life? He was interested in the interaction of the personal and the professional in the lives of others. Was this his way of expressing the tension between them for himself? Was he trying to confront his certain knowledge that there could be no end but death to his making of many books? Or was the paradox that, whatever Ecclesiastes said, the making of many books was not a weariness of the flesh at all for Michael Kammen, but just the reverse? Or did he simply know, as we all must, that weariness of the flesh puts an end not only to the making of many books, but to all human endeavor.

In some way, I feel sure, the Baskin painting was the self-portrait and the autobiography Michael would have wanted to make for himself — an elegant rendering of both his public identity, and his most private understanding of his life's work. Although made by another, the painting combines Michael's personal, scholarly, and aesthetic passions. It speaks with his now silent voice.

ALL PHOTOS COURTESY OF CAROL K. KAMMEN

MISSING FATHER

DIANA ABU-JABER

Your library was my lost land within your house of carpets, olives, oil paintings, musical instruments, snowy hills rolling beyond the windows. Collector of detritus, weekends given to garage sales and negotiation with elderly strangers, you were a fortune-finder. My father searched for houses, you hunted for their contents. "Deerslayer Country," the signs proclaimed; you read them aloud in the car, driving the long green hills between rural estate sales. Then laughed and said, "Oh that miserable writer."

As a kid, I felt prickled, unsettled by a sense of displacement — born to the wrong brother. My father had no higher degrees; he barely read English. You roared on foreign politics from a lectern. Dad went square dancing. You invited dignitaries, scholars, and poets to your table.

One Christmas, you and my writerly auntie gave me a first edition of *To the Lighthouse*. My parents gave me the toys on my Christmas lists, quickly forgotten.

I was troubled, bitten by it. The wrong father. I attended the same college where you taught and didn't always correct people when they assumed you were my parent. People called you "Professor." They called Dad, "Bud."

When you retired, you moved back to Jordan. You tried to bring the rest of us with you, but we wouldn't go, not even Dad. He missed his country as well, but he wouldn't leave us. Silence fell across Deerslayer Country.

There was no silence in you. You'd played your rebab, one-stringed instrument, the Bedouin thing, like your father before you. You'd kept your first country like a secret inside you for 30 years before returning. Bud let his go, in the tiniest increments, sugar dissolving in a demitasse of coffee. America increasing inside him.

Dad stayed with us to the end, relinquishing the person he'd started out as, until he finished in chino shorts and Hawaiian shirts, an American among Americans.

Now, people tell me that they were your student, how remarkable you were, how brilliant, what a mind. And when they ask what were you like as a father? I prickle and say, yes, I'd had the most wonderful father. And, very honestly, I tell them, I'd never really realized how lucky I was.

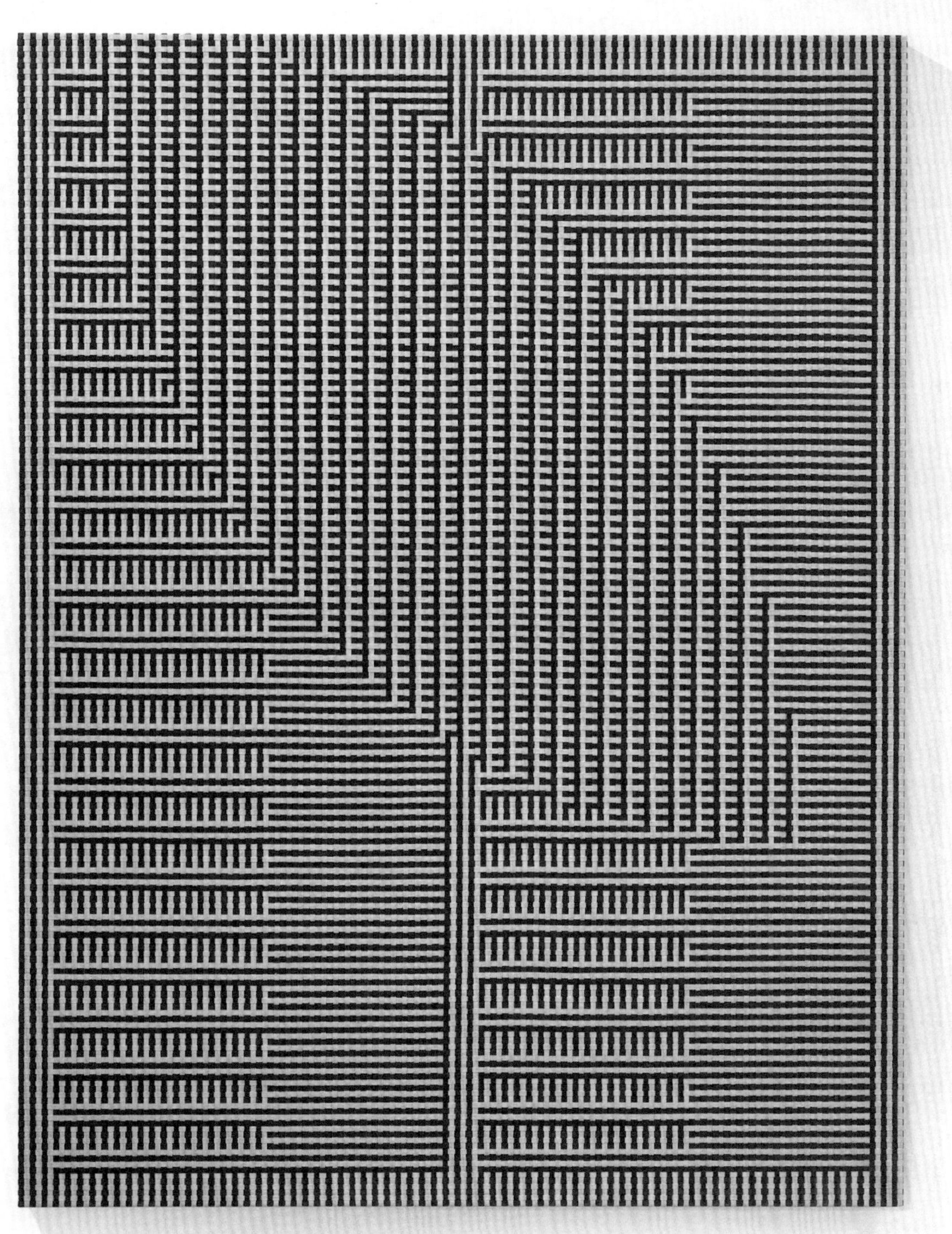

TAUBA AUERBACH, *SHADOW WEAVE—COMB / VOID I*, 2013
WOVEN CANVAS ON WOODEN STRETCHER
60" X 45" (152.4 X 114.3 CM)

RADENKO MILAK, *BODY LANGUAGE*, 2013
INK, WATERCOLOR, AND PENCIL ON PAPER
33 X 40.5 CM
COURTESY GALLERY DUPLEX, 100M², AND L'AGENCE À PARIS

If You Peeked and Saw Gaza

SESSHU FOSTER

Probably you were making love a couple times, you were getting busy.
Laying sod, planting trees, paving a walkway. Perhaps you called your mother.
Perhaps your child. Driving from LA to the Mexican border can take what.
The estimate for the bathroom, 15 to 20K. What's the weather going to be like, when you arrive?
Something about Gaza. The woman's car in the intersection . . .
You parked and by the time you got there, two other guys showed up to help push.
Rutsu 18, or Tokoro in S. Pasadena? Bombed out buildings like from World War II, gray concrete dust.
Gray concrete dust on survivors. The Israelis.
News on in another room; saturated arena colors of a flat screen in a sports bar, Washington DC?
Dim sports bar? A toddler cradled in a hunched father's arms, missing the top of the head.
How much had you? How much more to drink? Two or three maybe.
Phrase, tit for tat, something like that. It canceled out. How much money was it to you?
New appliances, developments in robotics, software versus hardware. Debt.
How's traffic? How's it look? If you peeked and saw Gaza you saw it.
You saw the end of your world, your own death in a way, the limit of sighs.
A breath, your own, and someone talking, saying something you didn't quite catch.
Hedges, fences and trees as you drive on. Houses, neighborhoods of night streets.
Little universes.

AUNTIES

RABIH ALAMEDDINE

Most of my aunties, my mother included, sat around in a daze under the hanging lamps, spent half their time in hope, and half in waiting, waiting for a miracle that never visited, waiting for something or someone to fly them out of their adopted life. Auntie Badeea, on the other hand, didn't wait for anything, she loved her life, and she loved me. Older than my mother though not by much, she took me under her wing, more precisely under her skirt — no, not sexual, I was much too young and she didn't have that much sex, in any case. That's why she had the time to look after me. She was dark and overweight, which at one point was popular with clients, but as Americans began to frequent the house, she was less desired, she lay beyond their longings. Though she went through the prescribed motions every evening, it was merely gestures, a performance for performance's sake, the motions included painting her face while the men were already in the room, she was the only one who did that. About one hour after evening prayers, she descended the unbanistered stairs into the salon, splayed herself on a duchesse brisée whose bright canary-yellow color clashed with every single thing in the room. Once completely comfortable, her heft proportionally distributed about the unusual chaise longue, a Rubenesque odalisque, she languidly applied her makeup, none of which was store bought, all natural, organic even, crushed fruits and berries were the lipstick, in a small wooden bowl she mixed galena and other powders for the kohl before her rapt audience, outlined her eyes with a pencil-shaped stick of ivory. I stood mouth open, eyes wide, nostrils flaring, enraptured by the theater, and ignored by the Americans who loved watching Auntie Badeea, were mightily entertained, made sure to arrive early whenever they were bringing a newbie in order for him to witness her great art, but when it came time to withdraw into the private rooms, they redirected their buzzard eyes, they chose to fuck my mother, they sure did. She was younger, prettier, drank Pepsi and Seven-Up, blushed easily, covered her mouth when giggling, and had just the right touch of nonthreatening exoticness, just a tad. Since my mother was busy most of the time, Auntie Badeea took care of me. Soon after she finished painting her lady face, she would put me in her bed and I slept long before my mother finished satisfying for the night. Auntie Badeea usually woke to find me inventing the most elaborate games while sitting on the floor outside my mother's door, serving tea to Sultan Ahmad who entertained King George of Britannica, and the latter so enthralled by my tea-serving prowess he wished to steal me from my master while I demurred and blushed and covered my mouth while giggling. ⁄⁄

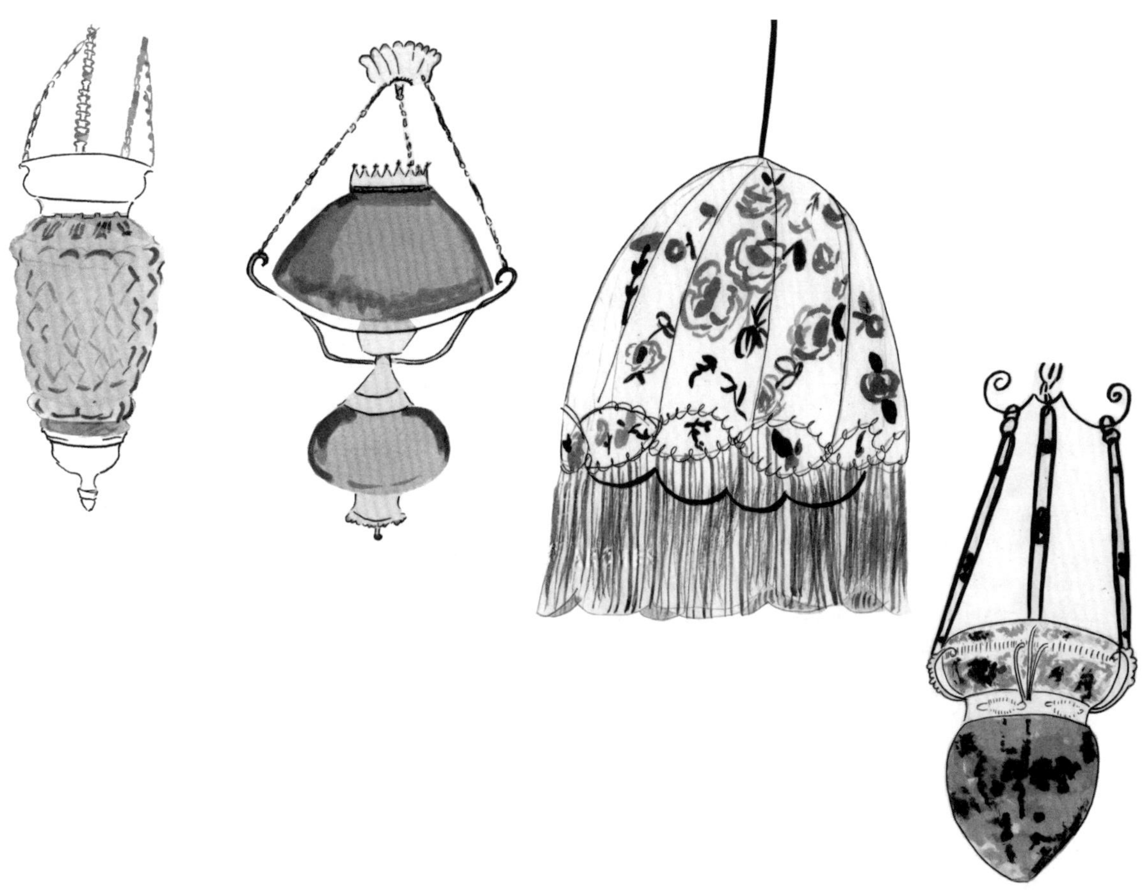

A GIRL'S GUIDE TO SEXUAL PURITY

CARMEN MARIA MACHADO

I was saved around a bonfire the summer I turned thirteen.

I'd spent most of camp making box-stitch plastic lanyards and climbing trees, but now the counselors — a smattering of high school and college students; a pastor — fed us s'mores and encouraged us to think about everything we'd ever done wrong. Around me, a miasma of grieving sobs thickened as other middle schoolers recalled their many sins. I stood up; ready for the fresh start I thought I needed.

A "Certificate of New Birth," presented to me the next day, was printed on thin, grainy paper and marks the exact moment of conversion at 10:20 p.m., well past my then-bedtime.

Afterward, I was the anti-hipster, as earnest about Jesus I could possibly be. I walked around with a patch on my backpack that said "Ask Me Why I'm a Christian." I wore a ring that read "True Love Waits." I went to church, and liked it. I believed Jesus was my savior, that he had a personal stake in my salvation, as personal as my parents' love for me.

Nothing bad had happened to me in my life. Not yet.

A year later, in my freshman year of high school, a boy — much older than me, but a boy just the same — took my hand and made me touch him. Then he touched me. We were in a science classroom with long black tabletops and ridged silver nozzles. He was just rough enough, and though I didn't want to — though I tried to pull away — he persisted. I didn't know I could insist otherwise. When it was over, I walked outside and waited for the after-school bus to pick me up and take me home.

Afterward, I took this event — which I had difficulty naming — and put it down as a lapse in judgment. It made it easier, somehow, to think of it as a mistake on my part. I saw him in the halls almost every day — which caused me to shake my right hand like it was burning — until he graduated at the end of the year, and was gone. *This what happens*, I reasoned, *when you flirt.*

My problem, I decided, was purity, or lack thereof.

My friend Karla and I bought a book called *And the Bride Wore White*, a guide to remaining sexually pure. Three chapters of *And the Bride Wore White* are titled as follows: "Satan's Big Fat Sex

Lies," "Satan's Second Big Fat Sex Lie," and "Satan's Biggest, Fattest Sex Lie." The book explained to me why condoms don't work, why everyone isn't "doing it," and that oral sex is just as bad as intercourse. The author painstakingly outlined her own sexual foibles and missteps, honesty that I appreciated. I was ready to learn. I read the book steadily — during study breaks, walking through the hallways, before I went to sleep. Karla and I met at her house and talked about the different chapters while her mother brought us garden-grown beefsteak tomatoes that looked like hearts. We swore to strive for purity in every way possible. No more touching. No more being touched.

My family and I were members at a United Methodist congregation, but the United Methodist kids were not nice people. They were unfriendly and cliquish in a way that I could never articulate to my mother. "Why don't you hang out with some of the kids from church?" she would ask me. She never seemed to understand the nuances of my social discomfort, and I didn't want to explain.

So I joined my school's Bible Study, populated almost entirely with the teenagers from a local Evangelical church. I loved them, even though their beliefs were more severe than mine. One week, a group of them argued with me that God doesn't *hate* gay people, but doesn't want them to do what they do. Another meeting was completely derailed when someone drew a chalk diagram of decaying buildings on the board to demonstrate to me how entropy disproves evolution. They had a certainty I envied. I both admired their zeal and was scared of it.

I was also confident they were wrong about these points. I didn't believe in a God who rejected love or science. I reasoned Genesis was figurative, metaphorical. I could imagine the swirling chaos, the madness that God would one day knit together to form, eventually, this classroom, with me inside it. Turmoil, gathered into purpose.

I had crushes. Crushes were okay as long as you didn't *fantasize*, as long as you didn't let the crush decenter God from your life.

There was the boy who I'd been in love with since the fifth grade, who'd played my husband in a middle school production of *Little Women* and had recently turned the corner from awkward to handsome. And there was the skinny Mormon transfer student, one-half of a set of twins. I sent away for and read the Book of Mormon — hoping to impress him with my ecclesiastical knowledge — and tried to learn Magic: The Gathering — a hobby of his — but it didn't matter. He wasn't interested in me beyond friendship, no matter how many hours I spent wrangling with sincere Mormon missionaries over the phone or organizing a red and white deck that never won a single game.

My problems, though, were more complex than unrequited crushes. I was afraid to touch boys — all men, really — but I wanted them anyway. And when my thoughts strayed into the realm of sexual fantasy — hazy tableaus of kissing, harder and harder — I apologized to God for my impure thoughts. Sorry, I said, for letting boys jostle Him off His pedestal.

I also sat catty-corner to a girl in English class. She had faint freckles on the bridge of her nose. We both loved the movies *Fried Green Tomatoes* and *Moulin Rouge*, and talked about them almost every day. I liked her in a way that made me excited to go to class, even more excited than I was

normally, but I didn't understand why, exactly. I had a crush on her without having a name for it. I sat behind her and stared at her freckles and imagined kissing her mouth. She was such a good friend and so fun and so smart I wanted to rise out of my seat and say, "To hell with Hemingway!" and haul her out of class — to some end I couldn't quite visualize. I didn't pray about my feelings for her; it didn't seem necessary.

Sometimes, I'd have nightmares that I died, and learned that the Evangelical kids' God was my only option, and I'd done everything wrong. I went to hell in these dreams, of course, which never looked like the Bible promised — an abandoned shopping mall in the desert, the dusty space beneath my parents' bed in my childhood house, the bottom of the ocean — but always felt eternal and lonely.

Although I hung out with the Evangelicals, I still dutifully attended the United Methodist church with my parents. When I was sixteen, a new associate pastor was rotated into our parish. His name was Sam Jones.

When he introduced himself to the church youth, I felt a kick deep in my pelvis. He was handsome — with straight sandy hair that jutted out over his forehead and a goatee. He was a little pudgy but only just. He had a wedding ring. And when he shook my hand, he looked directly into my eyes.

Turns out, I'd been waiting for that.

Sam was around a lot. He participated in youth group events, alongside his normal church duties. He gave smart, politically progressive sermons that caused grumblings amongst the older congregants, which delighted me to no end. Within days of arriving he knew my name and used it whenever we ran into one another. Sometimes, I would linger after service to speak to him about his sermon. He talked to me as if I was an adult.

I guess I'd been waiting for that, too.

Later that year, an opportunity arose to go to Lichtenburg, South Africa, for several weeks. Our church had connected with a local Methodist congregation, and was looking to run a youth camp for the church's children and teenagers. A group of adults — ten or so, including Sam — decided to go run the camp. My interest in my church had been renewed by Sam's presence, and I'd been more active ever since he'd arrived. The group invited me to go with them.

At home, my parents argued. They say couples always have the same fight over and over, and in our house there was a fierce ongoing battle about my father's relationship with his family, and the way they treated my mother. The fights were varied — shouting matches that carried throughout the house, hissed arguments over the dinner table, slammed doors that seemed to get louder every time. I was terrified they were going to get divorced. I spent my school days swallowing mounting spasms of anxiety. So yes, I wanted to go. Yes, I wanted to work with other teenagers. Yes, I wanted

< ALEXANDRA LAKIN

to go to another country. Yes, I wanted to be away from my life.

We left on New Year's Eve, and at some approximation of midnight — the plane and time zones advancing together into the future — I drank champagne with Sam in the flight attendant vestibule as we soared over the black ocean. When we arrived at our destination — evening, local time — I slept for a few hours and then woke up jetlagged, staring out into the dark for hours until birdsong signaled dawn.

I had never been so far away from home. All of us stayed on a sprawling farm outside of town, in the owner's guesthouse. The property was palatial, with a pool and a white fountain and a gate running along the road. The campers, ranging from my age, seventeen, down to nine, stayed in a converted barn. I ran an arts-and-crafts elective. We sang contemporary hymns and played guitar. We built bonfires and told spontaneous confessions around them, though the call-to-Jesus of my own conversion was absent.

Boerboels — a giant South African dog breed that resembles mastiffs — roamed the grounds. There was a new mother with distended nipples and a loping gait, and her children. We watched her massive puppies grow while we were there. The owner of the farm cultivated crops of sunflowers, and in the fields their luminous heads bent toward the sun. We had left a frigid Northeast midwinter. Here, it was summer. The land around us was so flat you could see black thunderclouds slit through with lightening in every direction; storms so far away they never arrived.

After the campers went to bed every night, I would sit with Sam and we would talk. He spoke of his faith, and how he struggled with his own imperfections — pride, and jealousy, and, his voice dropping low, lust. "I'm supposed to be a man of God," he said. "But I feel so weak. I feel like every day I fight against my instincts, and half the time my instincts win."

He put his head into his hands. I reached out and touched his arm, and he didn't shrug it away. When he spoke next, I felt the vibrations of his voice in my fingers. "I'm supposed to lead all of these people and be an example, but sometimes I wonder if I'm the right person for the job. Maybe it should be someone better."

This, too, was what I'd been waiting for. I had spent so much time with the Evangelical kids and they had never spoken with such humility. They had been terrifying in their legalism and self-righteous in their judgment, but I'd never heard such honesty about their own weaknesses.

"Sometimes, I don't know what God wants from me," Sam admitted. "As a leader, and as a man."

I wanted to cry. I thought about what'd happened to me my freshman year, how awful I'd felt, how guilty. I considered my own lusts and shortcomings. I'd been wondering what God wanted from me, too: as a Christian, and as a girl.

One night we took our sleeping bags outside and slept next to each other, separately, under the stars. I'd never seen a sky like that, unstained by city light. There was the Milky Way, starmatter smeared across the black. It throbbed like a pulse. Satellites spun past. Planets gleamed. In the morning, I woke up and, inches from my nose, a dung beetle pushed a small brown ball through the grass. I am normally terrified of insects but I was cracked open, ready for wonder. In the beetle's determination and slow progress, I saw beauty.

Sam and I would get up early and swim at dawn. He had a rectangular insulin pump attached to his abdomen. This vulnerable detail tugged somewhere strange in me. We played around the edge of the glassy pool. He would unhook his pump, and permit me to push him in. When he came up from the blue, he'd grab my ankle and drag me in with him. We swam around each other, circling. It felt special; pure, even. And a little dangerous.

I'd never told anyone about my sexual assault. I'd barely put a name to it. But when I came home from South Africa, I felt as if the protective wall I'd constructed around it had lost its shape: a rotten jack-o'-lantern kicked inward. I couldn't account for the sudden rushes of panic, the images that rose up, uninvited. I shook and wept as if the trauma was fresh. I couldn't sleep. This old thing was after me, and I felt powerless in its path.

On a rainy afternoon, I sat in Sam's office.

"I have something I need to tell you about," I said.

"Go ahead," he said.

"This is confidential, right?" I said. He frowned and nodded, and then stood up and closed the door behind me.

"It's just — when you talked about feeling weak —"

He didn't look away from my face.

"It's just that this thing — happened. Before. A few years ago. I was with this — this guy. A senior. And he — made me do some things. Did some things to me. I didn't want to. I was just — and this whole time I've thought, wow, I was such a bad and weak person but now — I don't know, I just. I don't even know what to do anymore. I thought I had it under control but I don't."

When I looked up he was coming toward me, and held me more tightly than anyone ever had before. I was upset and aroused. He felt so strong.

"Help me, please," I said. Anything to keep his arms around me.

"I will," he said.

My mother didn't like that I called Sam by his first name.

"He's Pastor Sam," she said. "Or Pastor Jones. Like you refer to Pastor Anna."

I did call Pastor Anna by her title. I adored her. She was an older, single woman, brilliant and progressive. She gave me articles like "Who Wrote Luke-Acts, and Why Did She Do It?" and wore rainbow stoles to National Conferences. She seemed like a woman who knew who she was in the most complete way.

But what I couldn't explain to my mother was that Sam wasn't just my pastor, he was my friend. The boundaries that should have been up between us — minister/congregant, adult/teenager — had completely dissolved. I would just sit in his office for hours, the door always closed. He gave me permission to swear in front of him, which I did, profusely. "Fuck that fucking fuck," I'd yell, new to profanities. "That asshole. That shitty asshole." Sam would watch me from his office chair, rocking against its hinges.

Eventually, he insisted on meeting outside of work. I felt a strange rush of pleasure at this revelation. I was flattered. We had, it seemed, moved past the trappings of our circumstances, of our incidental relationship. He met with parishioners during office hours, with the door standing open. But now, he met me at diners at two in the morning, and I saw his face in the reflection of darkened windows. Sometimes, I drove to his house and waited for him to get dressed so we could go out. If his wife wasn't home, he'd change in front of his open door as I looked and didn't look, and then we'd drive to local restaurants and he'd buy me hot dumplings or grilled cheese sandwiches and I'd try not to cry too loudly. Once, I fell asleep in the booth, and he waited for me to wake up.

"I wish I could go to a bar," I'd say. "And, like — drink. Really drink." I had never been drunk but I imagined it as a wonderful blur — the same kind of forgetting that happens in the moments after waking up, before your life comes rushing back into you.

"You're seventeen," Sam would remind me. He rarely mentioned my age, but when it happened I could see the gulf of time between us, and I hated it.

His words were a mantra I repeated in my head: It's going to be okay. It's not your fault. You're not a bad person. God loves you. God loves you even though you're not perfect. I love you. (My heart jumped, here, but I knew it didn't mean quite what I wanted it to mean.)

My parents continued to fight. I heard my father cry, an unsettling occurrence I never experienced before or since. My mother confided her grievances to me, disclosures that made me feel uncomfortable. About my own anxieties, I remained silent. My grades, once stellar, were plummeting. A concerned guidance counselor called me in about a D in chemistry. "You're normally a straight-A student," he said. "What's going on?"

"Nothing," I said. "Nothing."

And this *thing* that had happened to me glowed singularly and harshly. It interfered with my sleep and made me jumpy. I couldn't look at it directly.

Sam called it my rape, once.

"It wasn't a rape, exactly," I said, because I'd looked it up.

But in my head I thought of it as the littlest rape, a white dwarf star that had collapsed on itself and was burning, burning.

I wanted him. On top of all of this, I wanted him. I knew he was married, but it didn't seem to matter. He told me his wife couldn't get pregnant, and they'd stopped having sex altogether. Maybe that was what I sensed in him: something caged, unfulfilled. He radiated desire. I wanted to kiss him, I wanted him to hold me, I wanted to associate sex with something besides fear and guilt. I wanted my life to be shaken up, to go from being who I was to someone renewed. Carmen, unafraid of sex. Carmen, in a relationship. Carmen the adult.

In those months, hazy from lack of sleep and raw with anxiety, I felt like a calculator with a finger over the solar panel — fading in and out, threatening to shut off altogether. Sam, though, seemed to run on his own hunger. I wanted to be like that.

My mother didn't know any of these details. But she was not a stupid woman, and had her suspicions. One day on my way out she stopped me at the front door.

"It's not appropriate, with you seeing Pastor Sam all the time," she said.

"I'm going out," I told her.

"Not with my car, you're not," she said. "He's a married man. You don't understand, but it's inappropriate." Her arms were folded over her chest in a way that inspired rage.

"He's my pastor," I said. "My spiritual mentor. Are you really going to keep me from my spiritual mentor? What kind of a Christian are you?"

"You're not to go in our car," she said, backing up so I couldn't leave.

"You don't know anything," I told her. I went out the back door, and then went and sat in the front yard. I texted Sam.

Ten minutes later, he was idling just past our driveway in his Jeep. My mom watched me through the window as I got in and we drove away.

The summer after I graduated from high school, I turned eighteen. I was finally the adult I'd always wanted to be.

I wept the last time I saw him. I was going to college but I didn't want to be so far apart. He assured me he was just a phone call away. "Plus," he said, "DC isn't that far. Maybe I can come visit."

In college, I had my first kiss, my first grope in the dark, with a dull man who had a hell of a smile. His roommate had moved out in the beginning of the year and had never been replaced. He was in a terrible alt-rock band whose lyrics were laughably melodramatic, but he smelled like cologne. He felt safe. Afterward, I felt strange about encounter. I'd never done so much sexually that I wanted to do. And now, I didn't feel bad or evil or wrong. I just felt nice.

I called Sam. I went to the hallway in the middle of the night so my roommate wouldn't overhear. He asked me what had happened. I told him, one detail after another. He didn't refuse any of them; he listened until I was done.

"What should I do?" I asked him, the question slipping out of my mouth before I could stop it. Until that moment I'd been secretly excited, bolstered with the newness of a man's stubble across my face, hands that went where I wanted them to. But in Sam's silence, which carried a whiff of disapproval, I recalled the sin of it.

For the first time, he didn't seem to know what to say. Where there had always been smooth advice that felt right and good and clear, now there was reticence. Hesitation.

"Ask for forgiveness," he said, finally.

"That's it?"

"Don't do it again." He sounded tired.

"I miss you," I said.

"I miss you, too," he told me.

A few weeks later, Sam stopped responding to my calls.

I went about my normal routine, but his coldness hovered around me, chilling everything. Was he angry about my hookup? Was he — jealous? I panicked. Maybe he had lost interest in me. Maybe I'd crossed some invisible line, committed some unforgivable act. I sent him a few emails, spaced at what I hoped were ordinary intervals. He didn't respond.

A few weeks later, my mother called me.

"Sam Jones has been fired from the church," she said.

"What?"

"The rumor is, he was having an affair with a parishioner," she said. "A woman he was giving marriage counseling to."

I sat down on my narrow dorm bed and leaned against the white cinderblock.

"I don't believe you," I said.

She sounded faintly triumphant. "Believe it."

I called Sam. His phone rang and rang. I couldn't believe he could do such a thing, and then I hated myself for judging him as I would never want to be judged.

As the voicemail message played, a small-girl-jealous part of me wondered: if this is what he'd really wanted, why hadn't he chosen me? I'd been there. We'd been so close. He could have done it, and I would have, happily. "Call me," I said, trying to steady my voice. "Please. I need to talk to you."

I took a train back home. I drove to the parish house. It was dark, but I knocked on the door anyway. When he didn't answer, I went home and emailed him again.

"Please," I said. "Please don't shut me out. Or if you're going to, just tell me, tell me so I'm not dangling in this in-between place. You stood by me when my world was falling down around me. Please let me do the same for you."

His response was one line. "Carmen, I'm okay but things are confusing. I have to go, the library is closing. Sam."

I never heard from him again.

I found out later that he'd surrendered his ministerial credentials, left his wife, and moved from the suburbs to a small apartment in town. I heard that for a while he was on a landscaping crew and living with the woman who'd left her family for him. I tried searching for his new phone number and email — I realized too late that all of his contact information had been through the church, and was now unusable — but his name was so frustratingly common, it was impossible.

Pastor Anna had lunch with me at Red Robin near my house. I ordered a hamburger and shredded my onion rings without eating them. Anna told me Sam was very sick. I picked up a dessert and drink menu and pretended to read it. I didn't realize I was crying until my tears dripped onto the Formica table. "Look what he's done to you," she said. She gently pulled the menu away from me. "Just *look*."

But she couldn't know he had all of my secrets and he had absconded with them, and left me. I felt like I was deep in a fairy-tale forest, and he had been a confident guide taking me to my destination, the unsteady flame of an oil lamp and his instincts moving us through the darkness. Then just like that, the lantern went out, and I was in the inky blackness, alone.

I went back to DC. I studied photography and wrote bad stories and bad poetry. In my sophomore year of college, I figured out I was queer, that I liked men and women. After this, I felt like I'd looked over and saw another universe, another version of the world running parallel to mine. I saw a timeline where my assault hadn't happened and I'd avoided religion and never met Sam and knew what it was to like women from the earliest stirrings. I was still me in that world, but I felt like I felt now — grown up, after a fashion. Like I knew what I wanted. Like I'd always known what I wanted. I gave myself permission to love sex, to be sexual. I stopped flinching when men touched me.

I lost my virginity my junior year of college to heterosexual couple, friends of mine who guided me through it all gently and with laughter and pleasure. After they broke up, I pined for the woman. We kissed and watched movies and kissed more and eventually she rejected me on a beach studded with the clear bodies of dead jellyfish, telling me she didn't think she was gay. I ran children's birthday parties at a paint-your-own-pottery studio and sold glass dildos at a sex-toy shop near the Virginia border. I finished school early and moved to California. I dated a former Marine with clear blue eyes and anxiety about his approaching thirtieth birthday. He was selfish and stupid but devoted to his pet rats, one of which had seizures at night and died right after we broke up. I slept with a programmer closer to my age on our second date. He was gorgeous and technically brilliant and taught me new ways to come. I fell in love with him, even as he pulled away. We broke up. I waded through a tar pit of heartbreak. I kept writing. I casually dated a string of men. There was another programmer, a kind, gentle man who went with me to movies and slept in my bed and let me touch him in the pitch black of the planetarium. Then there was the astrophysicist who picked me up and fucked me against walls and warned me about the world's impending helium shortage. I learned you could have dozens of sexual awakenings, each one different than the last. Every time, I learned something new about my body, about who I was. I felt like I was making up for lost time.

I moved to Iowa and fell in love with a woman, a fellow writer who consumed me utterly, alternating sweetness and adoration with violence and manipulation. She made me happy. She threw suitcases and shoes at my head. She told me she'd burn down the world for me. She said I was a cunt and drove so fast I was sure we were going to die. She kissed me on the corner of the mouth and called me "pai." She grabbed and twisted my arm and said "We're fine, baby. Right? Right?" She introduced me to her parents. I locked myself in her bathroom as she screamed and threw her body against the door. The first time I broke up with her, she begged me to come to a motel where she was staying and when I collapsed to the ground in tears she leaned over me, pressed her nose into my hair, and asked if I'd changed my shampoo. I finally got away: from that room, from her. I took a trip back to California and hooked up with some exes. I sold most of my religious books and thought very little about Sam. After many years of trying, I went from being a woman who wrote to a writer, full stop. I sold one story, and then another.

I had made a forest of my own beliefs, and lived in it. Here's how I left: I stripped away the trees.

My first god was a mishmashed Frankenstein of my imagination, made up of scraps from the Methodist kids and the Evangelical kids, of my upbringing and my worst fears. Later, when Sam abandoned me, I tried to believe in a God who loved and still left his creations. I could not. For a while, God was a faint, hazy presence, and then even that evaporated.

In time, the trees scrolled back. I'd made that forest up. Perhaps I'd needed to go through it, to be the person I became. But to realize it wasn't real? That took living.

Now, I was still alone, but at least I could see in all directions.

Last summer, I was eating dinner with my parents and asked my mother how her day had been.

"I substituted at the elementary school today," she said.

"How did that go?" I asked.

My father didn't stop eating, but his eyes flicked upward at her. My mother is a fierce and mercurial woman, and I could smell the thunderheads gathering as surely as if my hair was lifting up from my skin.

"I saw Jennifer," my mother said, in a faux-casual voice that fooled no one.

"Jennifer who?" I said.

"Jennifer, Sam Jones's wife," my mother responded. "His new wife. She teaches there. She asked about you."

My stomach jerked. "What? Why?"

"You mean, why would she ask about you?"

"Yes." I'd never met her, not once. How would she even know my name?

"I guess because of Sam," my mom said. Her voice was frigid.

The danger was clear, now, but I needed to keep going.

"What about him?" I said.

The table jumped as my mother slammed down her fork on the glass top. "The whole fucking church thought you were the one who caused all that. They thought you were the one he was having an affair with." I sensed her emotions swinging wildly between protectiveness and rage, between defense and anger at a decade-younger version of me. "Everyone was coming up to me, 'We're so sorry to hear about what Sam did to Carmen, we're so —' Everyone thought it was you. Everybody. It wasn't but everyone thought so."

Then she sat back in her chair.

"And the South Africa trip," she continued, her voice a little more measured. "So inappropriate. You came back and spent all that time with him. I told him to stay away from you, but he didn't. God knows what —" She didn't finish.

"He never did anything to me," I said, and as I did I couldn't believe I was defending him. I thought about trying to explain everything, but it was too much. Too complicated. And I've never been one to share much with my parents.

She picked up her plate and took it to the sink. I still don't know if she believes me.

I emailed Pastor Anna. I haven't stepped inside a church in years, but I still think of her as Pastor Anna. I asked her about Sam. I tried to play it off casually, but she sensed the wound. I did not mention to her I was an atheist now. I felt as if that would be admitting something.

She told me he was back in ministry again, in a nearby college town.

I Googled him, and there he was: a staff member at a local United Methodist congregation. In charge of teenagers. I watched a video of him on the church's YouTube account, playing guitar in their band. He's a little older and a little fatter than I remember, but it's him.

I think sometimes about going and sitting in a pew there, one Sunday. I don't know why. To fuck with him? To see his face? If he did see me, would he understand why I was there?

I guess I wouldn't know myself.

I'm living with my girlfriend, now. She is petite and luminously pretty: a little Jane Russell, a little Olive Thomas. When she's thinking about something, she tilts her chin upward for a moment, tugs on her lip with her incisor, and then comes back to earth and says something thoughtful and perceptive. I love her. We watch marriage equality blossom in one state and then another, and then another. We read memoirs about the struggles of gay and lesbian activists in the nineties — our lifetimes, our childhoods — and realize how lucky we are to have been born precisely when we were; to have crawled out from beneath our pasts and found each other.

True love doesn't wait for anything, as it turns out.

I found my purity ring not too long ago, tarnished and buried in a container of bric-a-brac. I'd kept it accidentally, carried it through five different moves to three different states. It was never more than a few feet away from my joys and heartbreaks.

I took a picture of the etching on the band — a photographer's instinct to preserve even my most foolish choices — and went to throw the ring out.

I paused over the trash can. After a few seconds' thought, I turned around and tossed it into my jewelry box: a reminder never to make promises I don't need to keep.

The Big Sleep #3

MARTHA RONK

This was another day and the sun was shining again.

No wonder we're cooped inside - Santa Ana's in the driver's seat,
down the dingy side streets empty of shadows to slide into.

Or later on the lam, zigzagging from tree-top shade to tree-top shade
sidestepping the direct glare can't help a return to:

eyes as windows to the soul, so the guy said, tracking her
disappearing heels.

For him too a couple of Scotches. For him too, useless swallows.
The need for a weather-shift to settle settlements.
Like cement-shoes one's innards.
General Sternwood formed by *an economical smile, a wooden gaze*.

It's said identification with character is jejune, but who's it then
looking back
        from a mirror over the bathroom sink, rubbing a chin.
                There was no sensation in my head.
                        The bright glare got brighter.
There was nothing but hard aching white light. Multiple reflections.
        Unshaven.

TANYA HADEN
200 PROFILES WITH A TINGE OF REGRET, 2006
PENCIL ON PAPER
11" x 14"

MY NIECES

DANIEL HANDLER

I have seven nieces. This seems like too many to me.

Perhaps this is because I only have one child, but no it isn't. Seven is just too many nieces to have, like nine martinis or five sandwiches or 70 cast-iron skillets or a paid staff of 300,000.

I guess it's funny that seven isn't too many daughters, but it's because they're not all the same people's daughters. One guy has two daughters, and another guy has three daughters, and then a woman also has two daughters. All the daughters — my nieces — are different ages, ranging from little to pretty little to not that little. They're older sisters and younger sisters, and it's not too many sisters either, just like it's not too many daughters.

It's just too many nieces, is all.

Sometimes they come visit but never all at once. Some are loud and some are quiet. Some patter around asking questions and some sit at the kitchen table drawing and some scowl around thinking dark thoughts. Some of them like me a lot — these of course are my favorites — and some of them don't care much and at least one of them really doesn't like me. That's fine. It's too many nieces as it is, without all of them wanting to be closer to me.

I can't help but think I should get rid of some.

There are a lot of things I would have to decide first. How many and which ones, are the biggest questions. I don't worry about how it would be done, because like most difficult things in my life I wouldn't do it myself, just as I don't police my own neighborhood, or make my own shoes or telephone, two tasks likely done by someone else's little nieces.

So, how many? Two or three seems right, leaving the number of nieces four or five. It could be fewer — maybe just one less niece — but it likely doesn't seem like it would be more. Having two or three nieces, after having had seven, seems about like having no nieces.

Which ones are tougher. There are two or three nieces who come to mind immediately, which is, handily, the number of nieces we're thinking about getting rid of, but I think they come to mind immediately because they're not my favorites, and that doesn't seem fair. Why should they be the nieces gotten rid of, just because I'm not as fond of them? There's also the sneaking suspicion that they might become better, played out against an easier field that had been cleared a little — better people, maybe, or at least better nieces. But at best this is an uneasy gamble. It would be terrible to get rid of some nieces and then find myself unsatisfied, and wanting to get rid of more.

So perhaps it should just be random, but then there'd be a real chance of, say, the niece who makes up a lot of songs, or the niece who likes to help me squeeze the citrus into the juicer when I'm making cocktails, being removed. Nobody wants that.

Also there's the problem of problems. Like all nieces — like all people — some of them have problems, and maybe these problems are at least partially the result of being surrounded by the other nieces. So maybe, rather than thinking of myself, I should be thinking of others, and choose to get rid of the nieces that will allow some of the other nieces to improve. Then there's the matter of all the nieces' parents, some of whom would clearly benefit from having fewer of my nieces around.

Once you start thinking of other people you can hardly stop.

I try to put myself in someone else's shoes to think this over, but it's hard to imagine being one of my own nieces, having never been a niece myself. I've been a nephew, though. I had two uncles, both dead now, one who I saw all the time and one who I saw barely at all. They both seemed fond of me, but I was their only nephew; one nephew isn't enough to think about getting rid of.

I remember when I lost the first of my uncles, the one I hardly ever saw. I was in high school and my mother was very upset, and I remember looking at her weeping and understanding for the first time, with the dumb amazement of selfish adolescence, the very basic fact that my uncle was not just an uncle but my mother's only brother. It was what my father said, when my second and last uncle died: "My only brother." By then I was an adult who had lost many people, and my father was ailing; soon I was going to lose him. I knew just what he meant.

My only brother. There should have been more.

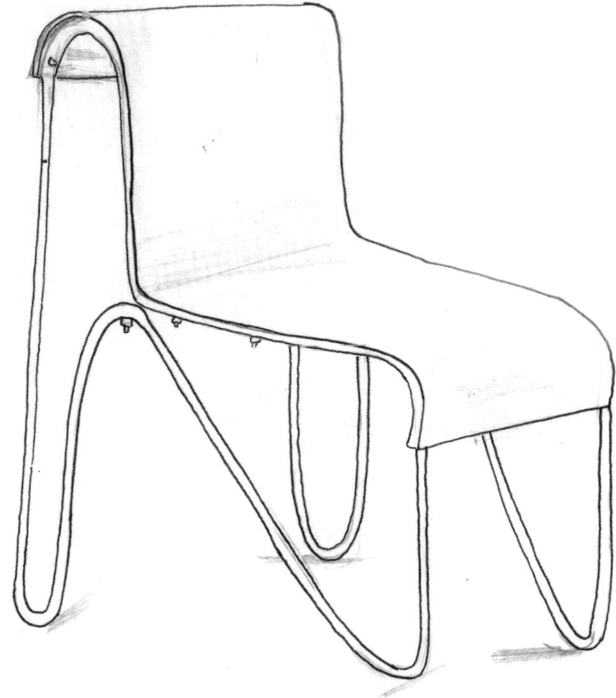

JOHN RECHY: AN INTERVIEW

JOHN-MANUEL ANDRIOTE
AND TOM LUTZ

John Rechy is an American writer best known for his novels, starting with the groundbreaking City of Night *(1963). He is the recipient of PEN Center USA's Lifetime Achievement Award, The Publishing Triangle's William Whitehead Award for Lifetime Achievement, and The Luis Leal Award for distinction in Chicano/Latino Literature — he is known as a pioneer of LGBT literature and Chicano/Latino literature. Based in Los Angeles, Rechy taught for many years at USC. He spoke to John-Manuel Andriote and Tom Lutz about his long and distinguished career.*

JOHN-MANUEL ANDRIOTE: **You mention in your introduction to the 1984 edition of *City of Night* that your early works included many poems. Something I have admired about your writing is its poetic quality — words chosen both for connotation and denotation, spare yet voluptuous language, cadence. Have you continued to write poetry throughout your career? Have you used poetry as a way to hone your writing? Have you published your poetry?**

JOHN RECHY: In my teen years, I did write some poetry (in addition to the novels I was writing). The poems were often in rhymed pentameter. I liked epic subjects: "The Crazy Fall of Man" was one, in which, at the end, Judgment Day, outraged people come to judge God, not the other way around; the last person is Christ, so powerfully accusing God that He — God — throws himself into hell, like this: "And raising his mighty hand in an act of contrition, God said, 'Forgive, forgive, forgive,' and flung Himself headlong into the bottomless pit of hell."

I wrote other poems, too, short ones. So, yes, in my prose I often write in pentameter, carefully. In all my books, I will very often add a word or subtract a word, or choose one with fewer or more syllables to fulfill the intended rhythm. I often adjust the prose to prop up action; e.g., during the

< JOHN HOGAN

Mardi Gras section in *City of Night*. In that passage, I chose active verbs, at times colliding to convey the franticness. I did conceive of some passages as "poetry." So, yes, I have "used poetry as a way to hone [my] writing." Even when I have chosen plainer prose to fit the narrative of a book (*The Coming of the Night* throughout), I will adjust a passage with added syllables (say) to fulfill a rhythmic requirement. Too, I will often banish adjectives of color to create a sense of psychological and/or physical darkness. I would say that my attention to rhythm has come partly from poetry, my own and what I've read; for example, John Milton and Alexander Pope — really — and the metaphysical poets like James Thomson: all are influences.

TOM LUTZ: *Numbers*, your second novel, seems to me to be the most penetrating analysis of narcissism ever written. Did you think of it as a book about narcissism? Or is that not the right term?

Yes, about narcissism, and as part of that the death of youth — which is what Johnny Rio is futilely fighting, although he declares his firm knowledge that he will never age, and that, of course, is impossible. As part of the theme of narcissism, Johnny Rio drives up to the observatory periodically to look at himself in the mirror, especially after some kind of "triumph" in the park. There is one time, however, when he does not see what he expects; he sees another image of himself, a somewhat distorted image that frightens him — evoking *The Picture of Dorian Gray*.

Another aspect of the same: Johnny encounters a man. (I believe he's driving a convertible, or an identifiable car.) That man recurs, and each time he appears he seems younger to Johnny.

Toward the end of the book, the man has become very attractive and young; and Johnny protests: "Why are you following me?" The man answers: "I thought you were following me." … Also, about halfway into the book, "the park" becomes "the Park," a player in the novel, pulling Johnny into its "lower depths" (literally; Johnny moves into the lower trails and "tree caverns" of the Park). Of course, there is "the Heavenly Sniper" that Johnny in the end futilely aims a "rifle" at (imitating it with his cocked hand) and shoots. Too, there is the title: gay "numbers," biblical numbers (counted), and, essentially, "numb-ers" — the attempt to "numb."

That so much of this was not even glimpsed when it appeared distressed me; it was viewed as a "sex book." Get this: the German edition was sold along with a card the buyer had to sign, declaring that he (or she, I suppose) knew what the book was about and would not make it available to anyone else without that warning.

But now a word about narcissism in general. It has a very bad reputation: It is almost a required adjective in media descriptions of anyone who has committed a horrifying act. Not fair. There is bad narcissism (that needs no explication) and good narcissism. The latter is good when it allows someone to feel so good about — yes, and "love" —him/herself that he is not compromised by another's self-confident achievements. A good narcissist can abandon the onerous demand for "humility." "Humility" isn't grand, it's depleting. I find it's harrowing that upon being granted a wonderful honor (e.g., a literary award, an Academy Award, and upon being elected Pope or President, et cetera) the recipient claims — must claim — that he/she is "humbled." No honor should humble one. It should elevate both the recipient and the giver, a proud, creative synergy. What is more arrogant than a false posture of humility. (A terrible confusion occurs when narcissism is mistaken for the real horror of megalomania, very different.)

J-MA: I don't know when the word "gay" was first used, as noun and adjective, but I expect *City of Night* was one of the first books in which it was used (if not the first). Was "gay" an underground code word back in the late '50s, the period of *City of Night*? Was it part of the street language?

Fine questions, but I don't know the specifics of the word. I do believe that word was used up into the 19th century (or so) in connection with "loose women," especially actresses (today, ridiculously: "female actors," a phrase I detest). I do believe the word became widely used around the '50s, but earlier more as the word of the initiated. I resisted the word; I agreed with C. Isherwood, who said the noun "gays" made us sound like "bliss ninnies." I've felt that gay men — yes, the men — often choose and propound terrible words to designate ourselves. The worst one so far is "queer" — and I shall never use it other than in reference to it. I have, only somewhat jokingly, suggested we call ourselves "Trojans."

TL: You once said *This Day's Death* was your least favorite of all your books — do you still feel that way?

This is what happened — from its inception, in my opinion, the book went wrong. The main reason, I believe, is that at the time I was writing it I was facing an actual trial (the one Jim Girard is involved in); I had been arrested the way Jim Girard is, in Griffith Park. I was actually faced with a possible five-year prison sentence, the same as Jim Girard: the vice cops, the court, the lawyers, the judge, the unbelievable moving of the trial into the sex arena of Griffith Park so that the judge could "see for himself" — incredible as all that sounds today. I used the actual transcript of the trial, but I had to alter it because the actual account makes little sense. … Then, too, my mother was going through a period of undiagnosable illness. I used those facts and created Mrs. Girard, who is not at all my mother, just another character in my mother's situations. *The New York Times* review appeared; my mother had just died. The review was odious. The reviewer had not read the book, and it was obvious because he wrote: "Why Jim Girard goes to the park is never explained" — whereas, in the actual book I had written: "And why did Jim Girard go to the park that day?" — a technique I often use to ask questions the reader may have. And I go on, in the book, to answer that in detail. I wrote a letter of protest, bringing up that point; it was published — and I believe that was when my enduring battle with *The New York Times* began, and continues. …

Recently, while receiving some honors at UC Merced and UC Santa Barbara and UCLA, I discovered that several astute professors admired *This Day's Death*. A woman who is writing her dissertation on my work — Beth Hernandez-Jason at Merced — praised that book to me and objected strongly when I told her I had asked that it not be kept in print. So did others. I still don't think it is "a good book," but I have deferred and allowed Grove to keep it in print.

J-MA: You explored themes in *City of Night* that are, to put it mildly, extraordinarily "mature" for a young man of 32, as you were at the time of the book's publication. For example, you were powerfully tuned into loneliness — and you saw, and described, loneliness as the driving force behind so much of what we do to obtain sex and connection with others. Ultimately, toward the redemptive moment of Ash Wednesday, you write, "My God but I'm lonely." It seems, in that admission, that our narrator has found his salvation, at least its possibility.

Please describe your relationship to loneliness as a young man and how *City of Night* — like the words of Jeremy Adams — offers "a hint of a kind of balm on the loneliness … a possible substitute for salvation"?

To write about "the gay world" you cannot avoid the subject of loneliness. As "politically incorrect" as this may be, loneliness is endemic — paradoxically most often in popular gay bars and dance places — a sense, in the dancing, of franticness to connect. Why this? Because, no matter how much progress has occurred — and that is a lot — we gay people will always be born into "the hostile camp" — that is, we are born out of heterosexuality and live — still — with the necessity to "masquerade" (drag, leather?). The emphasis on youth and beauty — both fleeting — are further guarantors of loneliness. Gay elders will often disappear, alone. (Or, forgive me, they may go to Palm Springs.) In several of my books, and in my life, I've detected, in gay gatherings, a kind of mirthless laughter that rises above the noise: a laughter devoid of humor, a laughter that seems to choke before it's ended. As great as the ability to marry is to our collective psyche — and it is great — I doubt that marriage will become widespread on our horizon.

TL: There is a recurring tattoo — a naked Christ — a tattoo that shows up in a few of the books. Was that a real person's tattoo? What are we to make of its conflation of the sacred and the profane?

When you use "real people" as characters, there may come a time when the real person and the character become one; I sometimes can't remember what I put into a book and what "really happened." Actually, I don't care — I think that's good. Narrative assumes its own life, and all "nonfiction" is finally "a lie." So: There was a kid — I think he was eight then — who lived in the projects, a sad little boy. I've written about him many times as "Manny." He was in and out of detention home and finally in and out of prison, where he hanged himself. I wrote about him for *The Texas Observer* and there followed an investigation as to what was his cause of death. (That is used in *The Miraculous Day of Amalia Gómez*; he appears in *The Fourth Angel*, and he appears in my play *Tigers Wild* and in *Bodies and Souls*.) That's all background. I believe that he did have a tattoo of Christ, but I don't think Christ was naked. That is one connection to a "naked Christ." More, though: I have always been fascinated by the sexual imagery in Catholic churches and religious art, especially depicting Christ. In representations of his crucifixion he is incredibly beautiful, his body is lithely muscular, perfect, and the loincloth covers him just above the pubic area. It is that figure that congregants are expected to kneel and "adore." That is the figure that nuns "marry" before. … And yet people are aghast to think of Jesus as a sexual figure. The sex scene between Jesus and Judas in *Our Lady of Babylon* — while Mary Magdalene looks on after having taken part with them — is one of my favorites, although, yes, it was difficult to write.

To me, psychological disturbances emerge out of the confusion with that naked figure, tortured, and the forbidding of sexuality. …

I have used those aspects as commentaries in my work; I have used it to depict the horror that can come out of it (an actual crucifixion in *Rushes* and an actual melding of religion and rape in *The Coming of the Night*). I have also used it for very broad satire, especially in *The Life and Adventures of Lyle Clemens* — one of my most satirical. Lyle is trapped into "performing" as "The Lord's

Cowboy" before a congregation of hysterical "Born-Agains" — and two televangelists modeled after the notorious duo Sister Jan and Paul. In my book, Lyle, on stage, evokes what an older woman, a sexy woman, taught him about intercourse, and he adapts those moves into his "slain in the spirit" dance — really, gyrating sexually, while the congregation screams: "Come, O Lord, come." In the same book I use the reactionary Supreme Court judges as nasty minor characters; e.g., "Sandra May O'Connell" is a fluffer for porn movies made by "The Renquists of Encino." In that book, I satirize beauty contests, the Academy Awards, Angelyne, Hugh Hefner's mansion (where a peacock runs amok); a main character is "Mr. Fielding." I dislike religion very much, Christianity in particular (especially Catholicism, which is what I was born into), and find it mean and dangerous — and hypocritical about sex. Those aspects, I intertwine into many of my books.

J-MA: **And yet there is an obvious and profound longing for God on the part of some of your characters — perhaps the ultimate "balm on the loneliness" — and you deftly use religious words and imagery (purgatorial purple dawn; resurrective sleep; tenebrous). I haven't seen other reviewers/interviewers focus on that, yet to me (who grew up Catholic) it's plain as day. In our 2003 interview, you mentioned that you don't allow your writing students to bring "mysticism" into their work, and that you don't consider yourself religious, as you just said. But I actually find *City of Night* to be a powerfully spiritual book. We might call it "incarnational" because it's through the carnality of sex that it seems we find either the possibility of salvation (Jeremy Adams, "Knowing it doesn't keep me from being part of it") or damnation (Neil, the leather man in San Francisco, contemptuous of "the weakness" of compassion). Please describe your exploration of the "substitutes for salvation," and the spiritual struggle for "the absence of loneliness" (Jeremy)?**

I do disdain all religions, especially Catholicism because I was born into it. Religions, Christian religions, at any rate, do offer redemption, salvation, et cetera — that is at the core of much of it: salvation. But when you finally encounter the hypocrisy and cruelty embedded in every one of those religions, you're left with a terrible emptiness — no "salvation." We look for substitutes: often, yes, in sex, lots of sex. Now I can see how intelligent readers might find a sense of spirituality in my writing. I would say, however, it is, more, the tenacious dregs of early religious attitudes. I use Catholic imagery constantly, and that might lead to a deduction of spirituality. The imagery in Catholic art, in its churches, is erotic and — oh, yes — very often powerfully, overtly sexual — the Sistine paintings at times seem to depict orgies. And a lot of sadomasochism, a lot. Yes, and look at the image of Christ crucified in altars all over the world. What a huge impact that has to have: a beautiful man, a muscular body, almost naked, only a tantalizing covering — and a kneeling audience of priests and congregants.

One clarification. About your reference that in my writing workshops I don't allow my students to bring "mysticism" into their work: I don't interfere with my students' attitudes about anything, including mysticism. Of course they do know my view of such. The only thing I don't allow is bad writing.

When I was in the Army (the 101st Airborne Infantry Division) in Germany, I was sent, along with many other soldiers, to teach, for 12 weeks, servicemen who had not achieved at least a ranking in third grade. That's where my time "teaching" began, then at UCLA, USC, and my private workshop. I don't consider myself a "writing teacher" but a "guide," from experience: warn about obstacles, identify them, find ways to overcome them. I also emphasize how damaging the fixed clichés about writing are, yet they endure from "writing class" to "writing class": 1. Show don't tell. Nonsense; writing includes dramatizing ("showing") and exposition ("telling"). We speak about "story telling," never "story showing." 2. Have a sympathetic character to relate to. More nonsense. Some of the most memorable characters in literature are unsympathetic. What they must be is fascinating: e.g., Catherine and Heathcliff, et al. 3. Write about what you know. Even more nonsense. That "rule" would decimate literature, from Homer to Nabokov, and myriad others. The only rule I uphold is: there are no rules — write about whatever you want to write about.

Also: I do not adhere to the tired exhortation that a writer must never protest reviews, et cetera. I tell my workshop writers always to protest dumb reviewers. I do myself — and write thank-yous to perceptive reviewers.

TL: To return briefly to the question of religion — in *The Miraculous Day of Amalia Gómez* you are completely, it seems to me, sympathetic to the force of religious belief in a person's life, the utility, and even the beauty of it.

That is very true, yes. But such a view belongs to my character, Amalia. I am very empathetic to the beliefs that allow human beings to exist often through horrible lives. My mother was deeply religious, and it got her through painful times. Because of that, I often prayed with her, the rosary, et cetera. I would never have done anything to compromise that. Too, looked at objectively, the Catholic Mass is very beautiful, High Mass. In a church that only Technicolor could do justice to; the statues of saints, Mary, and Jesus all look like movie stars. The ritualized services, the changing, the spraying of scented ashes — that provides great theater, of course. It wasn't until I could see those rituals as such that I could tolerate them. Yes, beautiful drama at the core of which is — alas — suffering and repression and cruel judgments.

J-MA: It's clear that even the young narrator — can we say John Rechy? — was moving through his own narcissism toward a rebellion (against those who make outcasts of homosexuals?) of a more lasting, solid nature not based on youth. How would you describe your lifelong rebellion — as a man and as a writer?

Truly, I've never thought of myself as a rebel. This may sound naive, but I did not expect that *City of Night* would create the kind of stir that it did. It surprised me. When I read some of the reactions (some vicious, the first ones), I decided to keep out of the fray. I was in El Paso at the time and a famous doctor in New York invited me to visit him and go to Tanglewood for the American premiere of Britten's *War Requiem*. I went, and then I went with him to some of the Caribbean islands — first Puerto Rico, then St. Thomas, et cetera — back to New York, in Riverdale, I kept very private. Even a greater fuss (especially among some "gay" groups) occurred with *The Sexual Outlaw*. Books were returned, sold under the counter. Again, although *The Sexual Outlaw* is definitely "political," to me it was a literary work that, yes, expressed outrage. Did that make me a rebel? I was invited to do a reading from it in San Francisco, with Allen Ginsberg, and a few other poets. Ginsberg went on and on — it was clearly his audience. Then I came on. Now, remember that at the time ('70s) gay people were objecting to sensationalist depictions of our lives — they preferred a much more placid view. (And tacitly but powerfully forbidden was to expose our growing emphasis on sexuality.) For the reading, I dressed overtly sexual — jeans, cowboy boots, a form-fitting denim shirt, and that caused anger in the audience. When I read, and the word "stud" recurred, a whole contingent of gay men stood up and laughed loudly (that forced, ugly laughter), and stomped out. I continued to read, and then a second contingent stood up, roaring with laughter, and stomped off. I didn't know exactly why.

The next day at the hotel, a reporter came to interview me about the demonstration — an African-American queen was the interviewer, and we got along splendidly, ordering breakfast in the room. "She" then praised me in her talk, and chastised those who walked out. Did that make me rebellious? I didn't feel so. A few years later, again in San Francisco, I did a reading with Edward Albee. I received two standing ovations, gay men and wonderful lesbians; and Mr. Albee was booed. …

I suppose, though, that by living my life as I chose to — that that lack of convention might suggest some kind of rebellion, but I didn't see it that way. It didn't seem even slightly outrageous to me to teach at UCLA extension in the evening, and after class go out on Santa Monica Boulevard to hustle, though one night, after midnight, I was standing without a shirt on a corner and a car drove by, circled the block, and came back, and the young driver (who looked like a student) lowered his window and called out: "Good evening, Professor Rechy. Out for an evening stroll?" The point is that I saw/see no difference between my development as a writer and my development as a man. I do hope that both gained from new experiences, newer views. I don't KNOW. …

TL: The reader who only knows you from your biggest books might not know what a gifted comic novelist you are. *The Life and Adventures of Lyle Clemens* is the most obvious example; *Our Lady of Babylon* is quite comic as well. How do you see your own relation to comedy as a mode?

I'm startled that that aspect of my work has not been viewed. Every one of my books, without exception, has passages that I conceived of as "hilarious." Most of those are also satirical. Miss Destiny's party that gets out of hand — "Throw his pants over the transom, Darling Dolly Dane," acted out, would qualify as madcap. …

I delighted in conceiving of the mysteries of creation being discussed by two polite ladies in a garden, in *Our Lady of Babylon*. I imitated the tone of early English pornographic novels in the book within a book. The Pope is quite hilarious, I think, and the descriptions: "her impudent breasts." (Ermenegildo, the peacock, is named after my favorite designer, Ermenegildo Zegna. …) Of course, the intention of the book finally is not only satirical (about God's monstrous judgment on Eve), but serious in its implications: God conniving to blame women for the worst debacles in history, the Trojan War, which I claim is waged to keep secret the fact that Paris, the epitome of manly beauty, is actually "very small hung." This is a favorite book of mine, in which, yes, I tried melding high comedy with high serious drama.

TL: When I had a chance to interview you seven or eight years ago, for an audience in Palm Desert, I prepared by rereading or reading all of your works, except for one — *The Vampires* —

because it simply hadn't arrived in time. Just in case we might want to refer to a particular passage, I brought all of the books onstage with me, and had them piled on the table between us. As we got started, I said — okay, as you see, I have all your books here, in case we want to check something — and you said, without missing a beat, "Almost all!" That novel is a good example of the way humor infuses your work: it is a hilarious, almost James Bond–like carnival of villainy.

Thank you. Yes, I conceived of that novel as written in "comic-book style" — everything exaggerated. Images in Technicolor. Exclamatory dialogue — and, yes, full melodrama: suicide, murder, incest — even voodoo. It is indeed very funny, too, it's very influenced by movie serials of my childhood: *Flash Gordon*, et cetera.

J-MA: **You write of ghosts in *City of Night*. After phoning a number of churches on Ash Wednesday morning, you say:**

> **The symbolic death of the soul [...], not of the body — it's that which creates ghosts, and in those moments I felt myself becoming a ghost, drained of all that makes this journey to achieve some kind of salvation bearable under the universal sentence of death.**

You write earlier, in visiting Chicago: "I pursued those streets as if hunting ghosts." This has something to do with Neil, and an effort to reclaim the compassion and pity that had been underscored by Neil's willful rejection of those qualities in himself. Do the "ghosts" represent remembered images of innocence? Did the image of ghosts appeal because we are "haunted" by those images?

My Catholic background was haunted with ghosts and angels, which, you are right, recur. You are very right about the connection to Neil, and the "epiphany" in Chicago's skid row. Yes, the narrator wants to regain his view of compassion and caring as opposed to Neil's courting of pain and humiliation. But I wanted to indicate that Neil's desire for pain and humiliation had its root in himself having been tortured. In Chicago, the narrator is assaulted by the pain of life itself, without any courtship. The frantic calls the narrator makes, after the frenzy of Mardi Gras, are simply a return to what falsely nurtured him in his youth; really, just wanting to connect with someone from another time — the priests who offered "salvation" — but it is not found. A central image of "innocence" is the reference to "white sheets," which occurs in the opening of the book and in the ending. … Ghosts? I do think we live with them. I believe that death creates "absences." An absent person continues to exist, the way someone who is away continues to exist. Death exists only for the living, right? — and so do ghosts.

TL: **One of my favorite novels has always been *The Fourth Angel* — I think in part because of the great, sweet innocence of those characters. And that trio, I feel, shows up in your work elsewhere, as in *Bodies and Souls*, for instance — are they based on real-life models, or some kind of Jungian, archetypal force you feel that arrangement has, or neither, or both?**

In *The Fourth Angel*, I used actual experiences as an adult and converted them into the experiences that the four "angels" have. All of their antecedents are adults "in real life." My mother, like Jerry's, had just died, and I didn't think I would be able to cope. I met some people (adults, in their 20s) who became my "friends." They had unlimited supplies of drugs — psychedelic (acid, mescaline), as well as cocaine. I needed escape. I took the drugs and it was beautiful, the first times — and it became hellish later. That is what Jerry is going through, and his friends are Shell and Cob — based on the people with the drugs. Manny is the only one whose antecedent is an actual teenager, the kid I've written about. The point, I suppose, is this: that we became like children, desperate — and so I wrote about children.

J-MA: Let's continue with the image of "angels" — used obviously in that book, as well as throughout *City of Night* and in your other books. Rather than the "ghosts" of our own lost innocence, do the angels represent others, external to ourselves, who become either the instruments of grace and salvation — or damnation?

Good connections, yes; and I have used angels both as demonic figures (Mardi Gras) and punishers — that is, the frightening angel that "freezes" Miss Destiny: "What will never happen, has not happened, and hope is an end within itself." (I'm quoting from memory.) Yet the woman at the Delta Airlines ticket office at the end is also suggested as an angel. (Indeed, I saw her as that, myself; and I asked her name and she said she was "Miss Wingfield," a name so obviously benignly angelic that I deleted it from the novel itself in that passage.)

TL: I've always thought the first page of *City of Night* has a very different sound than the rest of that book, and the rest of your work (ellipses in original):

> **Later I would think of America as one vast City of Night stretching gaudily from Times Square to Hollywood Boulevard — jukebox-winking, rock-n-roll-moaning: America at night fusing its darkcities into the unmistakable shape of loneliness.**
>
> **Remember Pershing Square and the apathetic palmtrees. Central Park and the frantic shadows. Movie theaters in the angry morning-hours. And wounded Chicago streets.... Horrormovie courtyards in the French Quarter — tawdry Mardi Gras floats with clowns tossing out glass beads, passing dumbly like life itself. ... Remember rock-n-roll sexmusic blasting from jukeboxes leering obscenely, blinking manycolored along the streets of America strung like a cheap necklace from 42nd Street to Market Street, San Francisco....**

To me this almost sounds like you are feeling the influence of the Beat writers, engaging in their kind of Olympian elegy, with the Dos Passos conjunctions that they adopted, and the Ginsberg/Kerouac long line — all of which, as soon as you get personal, as soon as you mention El Paso, in fact, disappears, and your own style kicks in. Am I making that up, some kind of anxiety of influence?

I do see what you mean, of course. That was not intentional. I had not read Kerouac at the time I wrote that, and I was not in that group of writers. The opening chapter of *City of Night* was the last one written. Or, if not the very last, one of the very last. (I forget.) That opening passage was originally about 12 pages. I intended a kind of "flash-forward." That long, long version was cumbersome, however, and I kept honing it more and more — eight pages, then six, then three — and finally that one page. I'm not entirely sure, but I do believe that virtually every sentence was originally a paragraph. … As a teenager I did read Dos Passos's *U.S.A.* and was quite influenced by it, especially in *The Sexual Outlaw*. …

TL: Ah! So what I was seeing there, maybe, was not a relation to Kerouac, but the influence of Dos Passos on you both.

I hadn't thought of Dos Passos in reference to Kerouac. I do, though, believe that Dos Passos's *U.S.A.* is much more consciously — and successfully — structured than anything Kerouac wrote. Hemingway and Henry Miller are often mentioned by writers of the time (1950s, 1960s); I was never consciously influenced by Hemingway — I never admired him all that much. Henry Miller I didn't admire at all. (When I was about 16 and working in the "call office" of a large laundry, a wiry little man and his wiry wife came in often and found me reading between "calls." They invited me to dinner, and I went. The wife went to bed after dinner, and the little man told me he had a smuggled (at the time) copy of *Tropic of Cancer*. He brought it out, asked me to sit on a comfortable chair, and he sat on the footstool and began reading a graphic sex scene from it. I realized he was trying to arouse me, but it actually turned me off. (I left right away.) The reason it turned me off so was that the participants in the sex passage were dirty and not very attractive. For me, a good sex scene has to have attractive people, or at least one.

About the "Beats," an aside: I was in El Paso, in my mother's home in the projects — where I went to finish, and write most of, *City of Night*. Late night, very late, maybe about 3:00 a.m. the phone jarred me out of sleep. I answered, somewhat annoyed. The excited voice announced itself, a name I couldn't place, and told me hurriedly that he was with a group driving in a bus about the country. He invited me, exuberantly, to come on out and join the group. I was annoyed and said something like, "You're crazy, you woke me, don't call me again." You guessed it, I'm sure; it was Ken Kesey and the magic bus crew.

I did meet Ginsberg later and visited him in Ferlinghetti's apartment. I regretted the visit, though, because I really wanted to converse with him about writing, but he kept insisting that I take my clothes off. Then the phone rang and it was Orlovsky, who then asked to speak to me when Ginsberg told him I was there. Mr. Orlovsky wanted to know how many pounds I could press.

J-MA: You seem sympathetic — compassionate — toward the drag queens, yet you are derisive toward Neil and the leather world. Is this because the drag queen, in taking on the female persona, is perhaps embracing the compassion and tenderness that are assumed to go with being female? While the leather is an intentional masking/rejection of compassion and vulnerability?

I have always admired drag queens. They are, to me, the advance guard of our liberation. The courage it took/takes to confront the world with an attitude that implies "fuck you" (e.g., Chi-Chi) to all convention — that is brave. Yes, I felt lots of compassion — no, much more than that — admiration for the queens I wrote about, not least Miss Destiny.

Obviously — I hope — I'm not talking about "leather" as in leather jackets that gay people use (including myself; I still have my classic "motorcycle jacket" intact); nor am I talking about the "costume" in bars. I am talking about the hard-core "leather world" that is saliently defined as S&M, and that I find lamentable — not in judgment, not at all, but simply as a manifestation of "gay self-hatred" (a subject very controversial that, indeed, results in various forms of anger). I point out that S&M is sadomasochism, and that it is a charade of the oppression against us: the "sado" being the "straight-playing master" and the masochist playing the gay supplicant. I am not talking from a distance about this. I had experience in the area, as I've written about in *City of Night* and elsewhere — so I do know about the "leather faction" personally. Years ago in Los Angeles there was a "gay auction" organized by Fred Halsted, who was my friend. The auction featured crawling "slaves," leashed, bid on by "masters." It was raided by the uniformed cops, and I thought that was the perfect metaphor: real S&M aimed at gay S&M, in a kind of mimetic performance of actual "S&M." My views of this are spelled out in *The Sexual Outlaw*, incidentally. The raid presented this graphic depiction: gay "masters" and "gay" slaves were handcuffed together and carried away by the not too unsimilarly uniformed cops, the real terrible "masters."

And of course earlier I talked about my admiration for the courage, and endurability, of "queens."

TL: You are now always listed in any accounting of important Los Angeles writers, and in any list of important Chicano literary figures. Can you talk a little bit about those monikers, those traditions? You have focused on Los Angeles, not just incidentally, in the way that Pershing Square or Griffith Park are settings, but quite consciously, in *Marilyn's Daughter*, *Bodies and Souls*, *Lyle Clemens*, and *The Coming of the Night*, for instance. How do you see yourself in the tradition of LA writing? And when the canon of Chicano literature was first being formed in the 1970s — maybe even in the 1980s? — you were not mentioned in those lists as often, the way you always are now. Can you talk a little bit about your relationship to Chicanismo, your identification with the movimiento, to Chicano/a Literature as a category?

My hope, my profound hope, is that I will be designated as a writer, an author, without the ethnic or sexual qualifier, which are, of course, legitimate and major in my life, but, finally, not in my literature. … Okay, that's my hope.

About LA literature: I think it's relevant to say that I love Los Angeles, a profound city, yes. I like to think that it's where God — if you believe the story — exiled the rebellious angels, and that accounts for its promiscuous "spirituality" and sensuality. It's a city in glorious Technicolor. I do think that may account for some of what is thought of as "LA literature." It certainly does in my own work, maybe especially in *Bodies and Souls*. Still, I don't really care about characterizing literature into strict genres. … I suppose a negative element is the cliché that "LA writers" are often disdained by the self-appointed Sages of the East. A cliché? Yes. True? Yes. I do think there's a lot of envy "Back East" for our daring denizens, and, yes, thinking about it — LA literature might be explored for its … I hate the word, but here it goes … for its recurrent "edginess." (Again: the place of exiled angels, "lost angels," "rebellious angels"?)

Now about Chicano literature: There was a time quite early when, as you point out, emerging "Chicano" groups left me out entirely, not even mentioned. Then, gradually, I started appearing, a bit like a ghost on the fringes. Now, thanks to some powerful academic and literary groups, I've been put at the chronological forefront of "Chicano" literature, since, yes, I was writing about "Mexican Americans" — being one myself, my mother Mexican, my father Scottish — back in the '50s — for *The Nation*, *The Texas Observer*. I was doing translations of Mexican writers into English for *Evergreen Review*, *Texas Quarterly*; the writers I translated are: Elena Poniatowska, Emilio Carballido, Ricardo Garibay. … I'm fond of saying now that it was more difficult for me to "come out" as a "Chicano" (a word I don't like) than as gay. … However, I found myself "exiled" at first by some gay groups, and in some places I'm still somewhat of an "outsider."

The fact is this: I've never been a cheerleader, and I never will be.

J-MA: If we can call *City of Night* a coming of age novel — I think we can — then how should we look at its recurring theme of youth and the dread of aging? In our 2003 interview, you said you were pleased with your appearance, accepted that the "older" man in the mirror obviously wasn't the 32-year-old John Rechy, and that was okay. How do you look now at "the frantic running that, for me, was youth"? At some point you stopped "running." How did it affect you?

I am still very much concerned with my appearance, to the extent that I continue to work out with weights, eat correctly, et cetera. But I am not obsessed with it as I was once. I am satisfied with how I have aged. I have, yes, stopped "the frantic running," and I am happy for that.

TL: Having written autobiographical novels and memoir, can you talk about the pleasures and perils of the different forms, particularly for a novelist whose work has been read in such close parallel with the life? Did nonfiction feel strange? Different? Forbidding? A relief?

Thank you for the great question. … Increasingly, or, perhaps better, consciously, I've tried to "erase" in my work (actually from the very beginning) the demarcation between fiction and nonfiction. All literature is a form of lying, and in the hierarchy of such, I view the autobiographer as the biggest liar for claiming to remember everything as it happened, whereas memory has already done its powerful editing. Next in the hierarchy of liars is the biographer, who dares to claim that he can "know" another's life. The most honest of the hierarchy is the fiction writer, who says in effect, "This is a lie, a fiction, and I'm trying to convince you it's all true. …" In my memoir, *About My Life and the Kept Woman*, I mixed actual — remembered, however imperfectly — experiences with an evolving novel; that is, the so-called autobiographical events are transformed into fiction within the same book. My new book, titled *Island! Island!*, I describe as "true fiction," based on facts that I remember, and intertwined with fiction.

And, yes, doing away with the arbitrary demarcations separating fiction and nonfiction has given me a sense of great artistic freedom.

J-MA: Finally, in writing about Skipper, you say, "Life reveals itself, if at all, slowly — and often through patterns discovered in retrospect." Looking back at your own life, what patterns have you discovered? Which of the patterns in your own life/history were deliberately woven, which were not, and what did you discover from them?

What have I discovered? I guess I'll go on saying there is no substitute for salvation, a phrase that appears in every one of my books; but what I may have come to believe is that what is required is to redefine the word "salvation," by pulling it away from any religious context. Then salvation may be found in living as good a life as the terrifying world allows. For me that now occurs when I'm writing a new book and considering it my best; also in sharing my life with Michael, my "mate" of over 30 years. I've often said that instead of committing suicide, I met Michael, and that has allowed me several decades more to create and to share in Michael's own creative life.

TWO UNCLES

LILY TUCK

To me he was Uncle Fritz, but to others he was better known as Professor Friedrich Solmsen, a philologist, a classicist, and "one of the last giants of the German tradition of classical humanism." At Humboldt University in Berlin — home to 29 Nobel Prize winners as well as to some of Germany's greatest minds such as G. W. F. Hegel, Arthur Schopenhauer, Walter Benjamin, Albert Einstein, Max Planck, Karl Marx, Friedrich Engels, the poet Heinrich Heine, and, last but not least, Otto von Bismarck — Uncle Fritz studied with Werner Jaeger and Ulrich von Wilamowitz-Möllendorff, both famous classical philologists. The latter assembled a group of eminent young scholars — Uncle Fritz among them — known as the Graeca, at his home to read and edit Greek texts.

In 1932, Uncle Fritz married one of his students, and, a year later, they left Germany for England. Then, in 1937, he and his wife managed to get to the United States. First, Uncle Fritz taught at Olivet College in Michigan before moving to Cornell, where he remained for the next 22 years, heading the Classics Department, publishing over a hundred books, monographs, scholarly articles, and reviews on Aristotle, Plato, Cicero, Homer, Aeschylus, Hesiod, and other Greek and Roman writers, and, of course, teaching. One of his courses, "Foundations of Western Thought," was especially popular and covered philosophical, scientific, and religious ideas from the early Greeks through Hellenism and Roman times.

At Cornell, one of Uncle Fritz's colleagues and close friends was Professor Harry Caplan. Unlike Uncle Fritz, Professor Harry Caplan was short, exuberant, and social. His field of study was ancient, medieval, and Renaissance rhetoric, the history of preaching and the intellectual history of the Middle Ages and the Renaissance. His greatest contribution to scholarship was his English translation of Cicero's *Rhetorica ad Herennium* for the Loeb Classical Library series. Also, unlike Uncle Fritz, Professor Harry Caplan was a bachelor and lived alone. Whenever I came to Ithaca to visit, Professor Harry Caplan told me jokes and made a fuss over me. He insisted I call him Uncle Harry.

When Professor Harry Caplan died, a letter he had kept for 61 years, dated March 27, 1919, was found in his desk drawer. The letter, offering career advice, was written by his college teacher while he was a student at Cornell and goes in part like this:

> The opportunities for college positions, never too many, are at present few and likely to be fewer. [...] There is, moreover, a very real prejudice against the Jew. [...] I feel it wrong to encourage anyone to devote himself to the higher walks of learning to whom the path is barred by an undeniable racial prejudice.

IAN JAMES, *ELEMENTS OF FRACTAL TOPOGRAPHY (FEVER)*, 2008
FILING CABINET, PHOTO PAPER, DRANO, FOOL, PAINT, DIMENSIONS VARIABLE

WRITING IN CAFÉS: A PERSONAL HISTORY

BENJAMIN ALDES WURGAFT

I went to my first café to escape my mother, not yet knowing that she had once done the same thing — escaped her own parents by walking down the rickety stairs to the basement of the Starr Book Shop in Harvard Square, where she established a makeshift coffeehouse. She did this while she was a high school student in Cambridge in the 1950s, when the Square was still academic shabby, still full of beatniks, decades before the place would be cleaned, covered with money, and left in its current condition, an open-air shopping mall with a red-brick-and-ivy theme. In a basement filled with slowly degrading acidic paper between slowly degrading cardboard covers, my mother wrote poetry, met with friends, and drank the thinnest coffee you can imagine. In college at Radcliffe, she moved across the street to the Pamplona, one of the few remaining businesses that's been in Harvard Square longer than my family's been in Cambridge, Massachusetts, and she would, in time, write her own scholarly books there. The coffee at the Pamplona has never been good, but that was never the point of the place. Even with a new coat of paint it still feels grimy enough to think smart thoughts. The Pamplona has a modesty that's getting harder to find as cafés — and, thankfully, coffee — get better and better. It comes from a time when we asked less of our amenities.

Decades later and just two miles up the street I, 14 years old, walked to a different used bookstore in a basement with a different urn of coffee kept hot enough to burn all flavor away — but not hot enough to damage flesh. An aspiring writer just as my mother had been, I wrote awful poems in a notebook with a green marbled cover that (I thought) recalled the old books in the basement of the Harvard library. Since I still have that notebook, I can now report that it just looks trashy. I had no idea that I was engaged in a form of auto-seduction; that over the next 20 years I would spend as much of my time in cafés as I could, reading, writing, and hovering between those activities — and eventually asking the question: "What are cafés good for?" Cafés took me through high school, college, the itinerant odd-jobs-and-graduate-school wanderings of my 20s, through the opening moves of my scholarly career as a historian, and, of course, up to the realization that I had only retraced my mother's path. Melville's Ishmael says that whenever it is "a damp, drizzly November" in his soul he "account[s] it high time to get to sea as soon as [he] can." When I'm down, and when I'm up, I go to a café. I've gone to write, to read, to see friends or to get away from friends, to have strong feelings and to escape strong feelings, to pursue a crush or because of loneliness, because of inertia, because of dependency. I've gone because I liked people, or because I was trying very hard to like people. And of course, I've gone for coffee itself, but it is interesting how quickly that can drop out of the reckoning. I've gone to be in public, and I've gone to be alone in public. Cafés were the first public spaces I chose, and as I continued to choose them they formed a through-line in my life, holding me stable across coast-to-coast moves, different writing projects, and different visions of who I wanted to become.

Hemingway once reported that in cafés he "was like a charging rhino when he wrote," noticing nothing but his target. Whether or not this is true, it conjures a familiar kind of authorial self-fashioning. For a kid with literary aspirations, to write in cafés is such a cliché that it needs no explanation, but there is the historical question of how the cliché got its stripes, of how the link between cafés and writing became intuitive for us. I didn't write in cafés just to escape my mother, of course, but out of the belief (not *entirely* naive, I now understand) that if I were seen writing in public, I'd be that much closer to being a writer. But contra Hemingway, I always noticed what was around me, and it has always helped me focus; without all that noise I could never recognize a signal.

I don't mean to suggest that the café is somehow a perfect machine for writing. Even if you find the right balance of style, clientele, acoustics, and coffee, the words still might not flow. Not long ago a reclusive artist friend told me he doesn't understand writing in cafés, that he does more good thinking and writing in transitional spaces like hotel lobbies, train stations, and so on. This rang true to me — I read books for my undergraduate thesis on train platforms in downtown Philadelphia, and I still have all the notebooks I filled with tiny writing during my first trips to Europe, on subway platforms in New York City, and on BART trains all over the Bay Area. I thought of the way transitional spaces can set my mind to wandering in just the right way. I tested my friend's thought by taking a notebook down to LA's symbol of late-1970s postmodernism, the Bonaventure Hotel. I rode the ornate glass elevators and sat on banquettes, looking at the koi ponds far beneath vaguely Orientalist concrete arches. I tried to let my eyes follow the curves of the space, and I did, in fact, get a few good paragraphs down. These are the kinds of things that, thankfully, the productivity experts will never make into a science — there will be good and bad writing days in hotel lobbies in front of the bellboys and the overfriendly concierge, and good and bad days in cafés, but the transitional spaces have the feel of freedom, the mind swept up with the movement of arrivals and departures. Sometimes stillness frees the mind, sometimes kinetic energy.

Part of the thrill of being in public spaces lies in chance and openness, in giving up perfect control over one's surroundings. That said, "anything" probably won't happen. There probably won't be a robbery. While affairs aren't uncommon, it's hard to tell — no one is likely to have sex in the bathroom, which is more of a restaurant thing. Divorce proceedings are also unlikely, and so are adoption ceremonies, rain dances — and once you work your way down a list of events from the unlikely to the likely, you realize that café behavior is fairly predictable, that this encounter with chance is a constrained one. In Los Angeles (which could use a rain dance or two), I try to avoid Intelligentsia in Silver Lake after about 10 a.m., for fear of the beautiful people and their very small, very beautiful dogs, and I go almost daily to Fix, in my own neighborhood of Echo Park, to write and be around other people who write. I know that I'm expected, and it's hardly the first shop where I've built this pattern. At the Diesel Cafe in Somerville, Massachusetts (right next to Cambridge), I was a regular from 2000 to 2002, and that was where I wrote the first magazine stories I ever sold;

I wrote my doctoral dissertation at Pizzaiolo in North Oakland (a restaurant with a morning coffee service), between 2007 and 2009, sitting there for two to four hours each morning. When I lived in the Village, I showed up at Third Rail three to four days a week, and I couldn't write there because the tables were too small, but it meant something that an Americano appeared not long after I did, without any fuss. I realize, more and more, that I started to go to cafés in a game of aspirational adolescent dress-up, and I kept going to them as an adult because of my desire to belong. Even though I like solitude, I'm afraid to be alone.

If after two decades of this I am still a little confused about what cafés are about, I am in good company. The history of the European coffeehouse, if we somewhat prejudicially chart it from a starting point in 17th-century London, is full of debates about the kinds of communities that can spring up in these spaces, and full of worries about whether or not they are good for us. Coffee and the coffeehouse came to London from the Ottoman Empire, where the tradition of drinking coffee was centuries old but the institution of the coffeehouse relatively new. George Sandys, an Englishman who traveled to Constantinople around 1610, observed the parallels between English pubs and the Turkish coffeehouses — although Sandys also speculated that it was not the coffee that drew the crowds so much as the young boys, who provided conversation, musical entertainment, and sex, as prostitutes. In London, the coffeehouse offered up as threat not the specter of male homosexuality but rather a different kind of dangerous male-on-male behavior, namely "wasting time." Coffee itself was often thought to be disgusting — a few of the cute names used by detractors were "syrup of soot," "a foreign fart," "a sister of the common sewer," "resembling the river Styx," "Pluto's diet-drink," "horse-pond liquor" — but even for those who thought coffee led to medical problems, especially impotence, it was not as threatening as the space where it was drunk. Some perceived the coffeehouse as pure waste, a corrupting influence on London society, while others celebrated it with a strange enthusiasm.

It might be tempting to think of our coffeehouses and those of 17th-century London in parallel, but 17th-century ideas about work, leisure, and social connection were not like ours — revolutions in technology, urbanization, population growth, and social change make up a formidable psychic gulf between our time and theirs. We enjoy both more time and a more urgent impulse to measure it. In our world, clocks keep track of a commodity. To grasp the immensity of historical change, start by imagining a London with only 500,000 people in it, rather than over eight million. While the early coffeehouses sometimes hosted what were called "improving activities," including scientific lectures — the scientist Robert Hooke, a member of the Royal Society, was a prominent coffeehouse lecturer, and in one particularly bizarre case, a porpoise was brought to a coffeehouse and dissected in front of an audience, in the name of natural philosophy —the culture of "improvement" did little to assuage the sense that these places were black holes for the productive days of men in their best working years. Indeed, one way to understand the coffeehouses of this period is to look at criticisms of them, as in one example, a work of satire called "The Picture of a Coffee-House, or, the Humour of the Stock-Jobbers," published in 1700.

The author of this pamphlet refers to the coffeehouse as the "smoky office" of a "crack-brained crew," who represented all social types but who, once in the coffeehouse, began to waste both their unrecoverable time and their money by trading stocks, itself a fairly new phenomenon. The largest cluster of 17th-century London coffeehouses was located right next to the original London stock exchange, in "Exchange Alley," now called "Change Alley." Stock trading and lingering in coffeehouses, reading newspapers and talking about the news, seemed like threatening activities, and for parallel reasons. Their concrete value was hard to understand, and they seemed to dissipate useful time and energy into thin air. There was some reality behind worries that trading would lead to loss. About 20 years after "Humour of the Stock-Jobbers" was published, the South Sea Bubble developed, an early and really ruinous inflation and then bust of stock prices. It was in coffeehouses that many heard the news that the bubble had popped. Stocks could plummet into the ocean much like the ships that the gentlemen sitting at Lloyd's Coffee House began to insure — the seeds from which the Lloyd's of London insurance company would grow.

If the Londoners worried about moral dissipation, about the collapse of masculine prowess in work, and of course about losing time, I share only that last worry — but I add anxieties about my attention span. If that term is modern, if a formal concept of "attention" arguably only emerged in the 19th century — call it the process of focusing consciousness on a point over a duration — it is nevertheless one of those phenomena that feels like a permanent part of the human condition. My attention, like my time, seems always to take wing and fly away, and writing seems like an effort to get both to tarry with me a while. The dream of focus becomes, then, a dream in which the struggle over attention, like the struggle with time's passage, gets suspended.

If as a society we are always finding new ways to be distracted and bored, we already have all the ways to *name* distraction that we could ever need — from the "wandering mind" to the "wandering eye" to understanding consciousness as a dance or a strange loop, all the way to the "monkey mind" of the yogis, an image I especially love. That image helps me express my distress at realizing the mind can be playful and sweet and vicious and nasty, and all at the same moment, like the animal in question. Distraction is no sin — any more than impatience is a sin — just a part of our nature. But this nature is not always easy to love, and maybe it's right to call distraction sinful for that reason. Nothing drives this home faster than the sheer difficulty of focusing attention on thought itself. My mind quickly snaps back to the people around me, their colors and shapes, the planes of their faces and the clothes on their backs. I catch the sounds coming from their mouths and from their cups placed gently (or slammed in aggravation) on the table. They give me something to hold on to. Once again, I need noise in the periphery and signal in the foreground.

Sometimes, when I started writing in cafés, that background noise was sexy. Part of my adolescent understanding of distraction came, predictably, from my hormones, and my first experiences forcing myself back onto the page — and away from people around me — took place in cafés. I remember one day in particular, forcing my attention from the shaved head of my tablemate (my interest in shaved heads in high school, like the mating dances of the birds of paradise of New Guinea, remains one of nature's mysteries) and back to Homer's "catalogue of ships" in the *Iliad*, in which I was theoretically immersed. Jonathan Crary, one of our best analysts of the development of attention in modern history, points out that the roots of the word "attention" "resonate with a sense of 'tension,' of being 'stretched,' and also of 'waiting,'" which I think captures something of teenage sexuality, but also of the libidinal character of waiting for a desired word, image, or idea, as a writer, of the way writing involves lust and hopefully loving as well, with all the shuttling back and forth between the physical and the mental that this implies.[1] If writing in cafés means managing the mind between distraction and attention, it can also remind us that creative energy is on a direct continuum with other kinds.

1. See Jonathan Crary, *Suspensions of Perception: Attention, Spectacle, and Modern Culture* (Cambridge, Massachusetts: MIT Press, 2001).

The café is a space in which our attention can easily threaten to wander, where perception plays with its negation. This usually turns out to be a refocusing, the quest for a new object, but in that refocusing there is an opportunity for something Freud himself described as the "suspension of perception" or *Gleichschwebende Aufmerksamkeit* — literally "equally floating attention," whose opposite might be "deliberate attention." He was thinking, in his Vienna office, of the problems faced by psychoanalysts who could be exhausted by days spent listening attentively to the complaints and stories and dreams of many patients at a stretch. He recommended that the analyst divide his (and in Vienna around the year 1900 it was *his*) mind across such a body of information, not getting snagged on or obsessed with any one detail, nor becoming numb to them through "listening fatigue." Much as the analytic office could serve as a kind of microcosm of the modern world, in which absolutely everyone feels overwhelmed by information flows, the café can serve as a world in miniature, in which the writer has to struggle — hopefully productively — with myriad distractions. To function there we need the wandering mind, but we need it to wander along predictable and constrained paths, so that we can watch distraction and attention bloom out of one another, each originating out of its opposite, something that Friedrich Nietzsche once observed about truth and error.

In 17th-century London, the anxiety was not about the attention span of individual writers but about the open nature of these public spaces. At the big central table no one could reserve a seat for a friend, and a tailor could end up sitting next to a banker, next to a day laborer, next to a doctor, and so on. Some scholars have used this openness as the basis to claim that the coffeehouse served as the cradle of democracy, as people from different backgrounds discussed issues of public interest and decided that it wasn't the status of the speaker but rather the quality of his argument that mattered. However, this openness was not universally celebrated at the time — some criticized the coffeehouse because of its *lack* of restriction — nor were things always so open as it was claimed. The Grecian, for example, was a Royal Society coffeehouse, and it's not clear how welcome nonscientists would have felt at the table. But anxieties about the café's openness actually exaggerated the degree to which these spaces were cradles of political reform and revolution. When King Charles II, at the end of the 17th century, moved to ban the coffeehouses on the grounds (excuse the pun) that they were hotbeds of sedition, his own ministers disagreed and helped to get the ban lifted before it could be put into effect. Indeed, in their view the coffeehouse encouraged political moderation rather than radicalism.

The patterns we choose for our days are the patterns we choose for our lives, and so early modern London anxieties about wasted time resonate with me because of my own choices. But what if the story of the café wasn't just about personal time, but about getting sick of what our culture makes of time? The appearance of laziness (if not actual laziness) can serve as resistance to a hyperproductive society. Within the cultural history of the literary slacker, as Tom Lutz describes in his book *Doing Nothing*, there has been a romance as well as an anxiety about slacking off.[2] I know that when I'm at the café I'm caught up in both. I sit each day in a space associated with both productivity and waste, with focus and dissipation, with community and anomie — good and bad versions of publicness. Lutz describes the paradox of writers, like Walt Whitman, loving to let things go slack just as much as they loved hard work. In fact they often concealed their love of the latter behind a public show of the former. Whitman once said, approvingly, that "Adam was a loafer, and so were all the philosophers."

---

2. See Tom Lutz, *Doing Nothing: A History of Loafers, Loungers, Slackers, and Bums in America* (New York: Farrar, Straus and Giroux, 2006).

In the case of many of these writers (and I identify with this) it seems that they're caught between desires, feeling the pull of ambition on the one hand and relaxed pleasure on the other — or, more darkly, between the desire to create and a resignation toward entropy, between *eros* and *thanatos*, as Freud would want us to say. Either way, they want nothing of the world of commodified workdays, somewhere between the implacable refusal of Melville's Bartleby and a Gen X rebellion so ably expressed by the fictional character Lloyd Dobler:

I don't want to sell anything, buy anything, or process anything as a career. I don't want to sell anything bought or processed, or buy anything sold or processed, or process anything sold, bought, or processed, or repair anything sold, bought, or processed. You know, as a career, I don't want to do that.

Dobler, in the 1989 movie *Say Anything*, loves kickboxing ("a new sport, but I think it's got a good future"), and he loves his girlfriend-in-potentia Diane Court, and he doesn't want to become a working stiff — Dobler knows that, as Theodor Adorno put it, "free time is shackled to its opposite." If Dobler is very lucky he'll teach martial arts for a living, combining work and love, much as I struggle to do in the café, but then he must worry — as all working artists, and, yes, academics, must worry — about whether or not the love of craft will survive such an arrangement.

The prevailing winds have shifted several times since Generation X was in its first phase of rebellion against work. Now it is a rare privilege for creative types to have stable jobs of any kind, and free time gets dressed up with disturbing neologisms like "funemployment," a sugar coating that does little to mask bitterness. But Adorno's point was that in our society free time isn't really free. It is part of a system of commodified labor, and if it looks like the "fun" part of that system, it is the part that lets the steam escape so that the machine doesn't explode, so that everyone is well rested enough to get back to work. When we're at work, we should be attentive. To *get* attentive, we have to be playfully distracted. The café can, if we're good observers of ourselves, teach us not only that perfect attention is impossible (something office work already teaches us; indeed, offices teach us that distraction is a form of resistance against the ridiculous demand that we sit there) — the café can teach us that distraction isn't the enemy of attention but rather its constant companion. To banish distraction would cost us the very productivity that many wish to maximize.

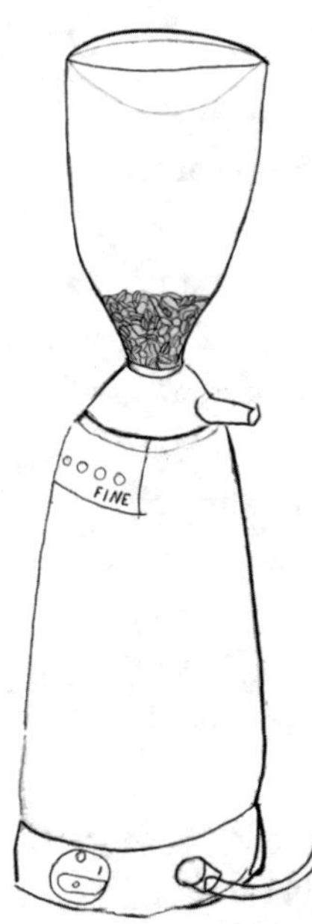

The café could never make me into a writer on its own, any more than it made my mother into one. (An anthropologist, she became a scholar of Japanese coffeehouse culture, and of much more besides, and it has been my privilege to join her in Kyoto cafés in the course of her research.) On reflection, I might have found ways to be worried, fretful, ambitious, delighted, and lazy in the library almost as easily. But cafés are more open to intention. To write in them, to embrace the play of attention and distraction, is to travel at modernity's pace while making very few physical movements, and to contemplate a quintessentially modern struggle over the meaning of our time, our experience. It means hoping that attention, either toward our writing, toward our neighbors, or toward ourselves, might thicken time and slow it for us. And it means contemplating all this not alone, not in silence, but in a social space full of constrained chaos, full of all kinds of desires, including the desire to write our days.

UNCLE WES

MICHELLE HUNEVEN

He was my father's baby brother, an unwanted third child in a difficult marriage. His mother drank gin, and threw herself down some stairs early in the pregnancy, then lived in guilt for the rest of her life. Today, doctors would say that nothing she did caused how he was. Then, he was called feeble-minded. Later, in his early 20s, the voices came on.

He wasn't severely impaired. He could read. He and his mother put in a marvelous acre-large garden with shade and fruit trees, a pond, a lath house for shade plants, and specimen collections of cacti, succulents, irises and chrysanthemums. Wes ice-skated into adulthood. He took the bus down to the rink in the Pasadena civic center, and he took the bus back. He also collected coins and stamps, although his organization was never strong; I have the collections now, two suitcases of stamps stuffed willy-nilly into envelopes and albums, one full of stiff cardboard coin books where, for example, the album for buffalo nickels is randomly filled with Jefferson heads from the mid-1950s on.

He was 25 and on the bus heading home from skating one night when a young woman started talking to him. He had a great shock of brown hair. A handsome craggy face. He was shy and sweet to people, always a little surprised — breathless — when anyone addressed him. The woman asked him questions, and smiled, and touched his arm, looked into his eyes. When she got off the bus, he followed her. She became frightened and yelled for him to leave her alone. He became frightened and wanted her to stop yelling. He pushed her down and sat on her.

She, herself, said it wasn't rape; but she'd been afraid for her life. He said he just wanted her to stop screaming. The judge sent him to the state hospital in Camarillo for two years.

This was right after my parents married. Every weekend, my father drove my grandmother to Camarillo, 60 miles each way. My mother often went along. When my older sister was born, Wes held her, then wouldn't hand her back. He held on hard, and she screamed, and he got scared and didn't know how to stop what he was doing. When my grandmother tried to intervene, he pushed her roughly. An orderly had to intervene. My mother never went to Camarillo again. She never fully forgave Wes. He was never allowed to hold me.

Eventually, he came home to Altadena, where he lived with his parents around the corner from where I lived with mine. He took his pills and functioned — with occasional eruptions. He made a small living as a gardener. You could see him riding around the neighborhood on his bicycle, with his lawn mower attached by rope, trailing behind. To this day, people I've never met before will tell me that he'd worked for them for years. Many of his neighbors and customers, whenever they received a letter from overseas, brought him the stamped envelope. In his stamp collection there are bundles of empty envelopes and postcards addressed to people, now long dead, who once populated the neighborhood where I grew up.

My grandmother died first. Wes and my grandfather descended into bachelor squalor. When I was eight or so I went into Wes's bedroom. His pillow had no case, and in the deep hollow where his head rested, the striped ticking was as black as burnt toast. I was horrified: this was life without a mother.

Sometimes the neighborhood kids picked on him. Or a customer didn't pay him, or paid him a quarter. He would ride over to our house; I could tell by the way he dumped his bicycle in the carport that he was "on the rampage." Yelling, swearing, and vowing to hurt people, he would pound on our front door, which sent a terrible thundering throughout our small house. My mother retreated into her room, my sister into hers, and I into mine — we never huddled together, and never talked about it. My father would go out to Wes and "let him blow," then give him aspirin and a glass of water. My father said Wes needed these periodic "catharses."

GINA MARIE NAPOLITAN, *THE IMMIGRANTS* (HISTORICAL OUTAKES SERIES)
FOUND PHOTOGRAPH COLLAGE

Because of Wes and his rampages, we girls were never left alone in the house. We were given to understand that he could cause us serious harm — what kind of harm was never made clear. When I was 16, my parents went to Japan and found house sitters to be there with me. But I was home one day by myself when Wes's bicycle crashed into the carport. As he yelled and pummeled the door, the door gasped open at each blow — I had neglected to pull it firmly shut, let alone lock it.

Terrified, I crept down the front hall. Wes, Wes, I said into the opening. Dad's not here. Dad's in Japan.

Oh, he said. Oh, that's right, Bud's in Japan.

Sudden quiet.

May I give you an aspirin? I said. Would you like a glass of water? Do you want to come in?

No, no. I'm sorry to bother you, he said. I forgot Bud's in Japan.

He refused to stay, and took off on his bike, lawn mower fishtailing behind him.

I was never afraid of him again.

GINA MARIE NAPOLITAN, *464 ASH STREET*

The Big Sleep #4

MARTHA RONK

Description's never the point given the gun to come. Can't hold up its end of the bargain. Still, it's perpetuity, not causality that counts, holds up after plots are long gone.

Sticks around after Silver-Wig's
never seen again, her kisses followed by, *You son of a bitch.*

The name's still La Brea, the eucalyptus still fringes the rutted road and the dust layers our overbuilt and guilty pleasures.

Parking lots turn over in their graves.

Night comes down as hard.

And the moon holds us in its grip, makes the windows what they are
when it's dark and we all go there.

We take in its shape as he offers it up, fitted to the ruinous city we know and mind somewhat less that nothing so far has happened.

A moon half gone from the full glowed through a ring of mist among the high branches of the eucalyptus trees on Laverne Terrace.

ANNE TRUITT IN HER TWINING COURT STUDIO, WASHINGTON, DC, 1962.
PHOTO © WWW.ANNETRUITT.ORG/THE BRIDGEMAN ART LIBRARY

MUSICAL STRINGS INFINITELY RESONATE

RAVI MANGLA

More than merely recounting the days, the familiar vagaries of the creative process, the journals of Anne Truitt are — like her sculptures — elegantly wrought and finely colored constructions, each book a uniquely edifying reading experience. In a precise and lyrical prose, she presents her person in all its hues: Anne Truitt the mother, Anne Truitt the sculptor, Anne Truitt the woman. Her experiences and perceptions are related with a humility and equanimity decidedly rare in artists of her standing. In an early entry from *Daybook* (1982) she articulates her ambivalence toward the title of artist:

> In skirting the role of the artist, I now begin to think that I have made too wide a curve, that I have deprived myself of a certain strength. Indeed, I am not sure that I can grow as an artist until I can bring myself to accept that I am one. [...] Even to write it makes me feel deeply uneasy. I am, I feel, not good enough to be an artist. And this leads me to wonder whether my distaste for the inflated social definition of the artist is not an inverse reflection of secret pride. Have I haughtily rejected the inflation on the outside while entertaining it on the inside?

The events in *Daybook* (a new edition of which was released late last year) come on the heels of her first retrospective exhibition, with Truitt balancing her responsibilities as a mother with her professional ambitions. In *Turn* (1986), Truitt adjusts to changing conditions in her home situation, the maturation of her children, and the quiet realization that her life has entered its final act. *Prospect* (1996), perhaps the most reflective and ponderous of the trio, has Truitt looking back on the body of her work, and on the fruits of a career she hadn't anticipated. Although contemplative by nature, these books aren't without eventful moments — such as when her austere, monochromatic *Arundel* paintings incite a public campaign against the Baltimore Museum of Art — or familial dramas, as when her youngest son, Samuel, is hospitalized after a serious car accident.

Truitt is best known for her tall, columnar sculptures, which first caught the attention of art critic Clement Greenberg in the mid-1960s. Alternately grouped with the Washington Color and the early Minimalists, she resists the conventions of either party. Her meticulous layering of color and rejection of industrial process align her more closely with Abstract Expressionists like Ad Reinhardt and Barnett Newman than her immediate contemporaries. At one point in *Prospect*, in what might be seen as an eschewal of the minimalist sticker, she remarks on the physical appearance of her pieces: "I walk around these sculptures in my mind and consider their existence. They look so objective. Yet each one sprang from the very core of my subjectivity." For this reason it is not unwarranted to think of Anne Truitt as sui generis, as a movement unto herself.

A latecomer to the written word, Truitt takes to writing like a pigeon to power line. Had she not fallen under the spell of the visual arts, one suspects she could have flourished into an essayist in the mold of Joan Didion or Cynthia Ozick, and of that order. She delights in putting words to complicated metaphysical ideas and has a knack for drawing out the unique spirit of her surroundings. Her flair for language is on full display in this selection from *Prospect*, in which she and a fellow artist take a road trip through the Canadian countryside:

> In Alberta, we turned south off the highway and meandered for a whole day on narrow dirt roads interconnecting the few inhabitants of wheat and grazing land. Their houses and barns were often painted bright red — heartening against the winter snow, and even in the brilliant sunshine of a summer day declaring the intention of indomitability. It would take a store of courage to live on land that so emphatically does not need a human hand. Deserted homesteads, abandoned to sky and wind, were skeletons of failure. Hour after hour, day after day, the men and women who live there must wrestle with the fact that even their best effort can ultimately have only the most fleeting effect on the remorseless roll of these spaces. They may have fallen in love with the prairie, as sailors fall in love with the sea.
>
> We stopped to listen to the wind, a hypnotic sweet sound borne on the sway of the grasses, musical strings infinitely resonant.
>
> "Would we," I asked John as we stood knee-deep, listening, our hair lifting into the cool blue air, "have been moved to art if we had been born on this prairie?"
>
> He tilted his head. "That's a question."

To read these journals in succession, from start to finish, is akin to being carried along a slow rolling sea. Each entry in the series is, like her impressions of the prairie, a self-contained wonder of astonishing beauty and breadth. Her sculptures may be her legacy, but her journals are her largesse, a gift from which future generations of creators can derive the inspiration and guidance they require to continue down their solitary road.

ANNE TRUITT >
COME UNTO THESE YELLOW SANDS II, 1979
ACRYLIC ON WOOD
COURTESY OF MATTHEW MARKS GALLERY AND BRIDGEMAN IMAGES

During a wildfire in Santa Barbara,
the high wind carries a single tendril of smoke
into a delicate loop, fragile as the
three-legged dog
limping towards the back
of the clinic after sixteen
years of loyalty.
The murderer,
strapped upright
in the wooden chair,
whispers a prayer
for forgiveness after the executioner
gently sponges his head.
The victim's family
watches through glass
too thick to carry
whispers.
In Kansas City,
a boy
borrows his
neighbor's
lawnmower
without asking.
He's beaten
until his skin swells like
tulips in full bloom,
mosquitoes drunk on blood.
The sun sets, casting
its glare on his dying
brown skin.
Every cell in my body
contains atomic potential
as I throw myself like Buster Keaton
across the world's stage.
Today,
while criss-crossing the New York skyline,
I stop a kid from
shoplifting Hustler.
GRACE

The Death of the Golden Avenger
Upon finding the body, The Atomic Man gently unties
the belt and lets everything fall
into place. He considers what's best
for the body, for the news sure to come.
The people who will hear it,
the boys and girls, the brand –
The sun is a burnt orange
peel in the sky, slicing through curtains,
casting slivers of rind on the hardwood floor.
There is no way to know this.
Some say he whispers a prayer for strength.
Others claim he prays to no god,
he simply wills himself
to act, like all men do
when facing the dark water of the world.
He feels the bridge of the nose snap against
his knuckles.
The rest becomes easy.
He rips clothes,
breaks bones,
burns flesh.
He cradles the head
in his arms and twists.
It pulls away
quickly, like a girl tearing taffy with her teeth,
her mouth full of orange,
the inside of flame.

Whenever there's Danger,
She calls the Thunder,
transforms into me, her secret avatar.
One moment she's walking to school,
the next
I'm rocketing down 3rd street
after the break-less bus,
halting steel with bare hands.
Late nights she creeps out the bedroom window,
the cacophony of cicadas witness the thunder.
I return at dawn in tired flesh, lacerated
with sweat and blood. We share nothing
but a body. In her waking
I'm a dream's veil away. I know
where she lives, her mother's maiden name,
the boy she longs to give her first kiss.
Ms Fortune's
Badassss Song
She knows my name from headlines:
Ms. Fortune Foils Bank Robbery!
I'm a repressed memory.
the recollection of hauling a lava
monster into the sun
like an itch in the back of her throat.
something
better forgotten when the day is hers –
What will I do when she grows into a
Woman
naturally by age
instead of by absurd design?
Call the thunder no more.

Prodigy
By the time morning breaks through
our bedroom window,
I'm on my third glass,
wishing I could feel brandy
the way a man was supposed to.
I should be half-drowsed,
only a dull sense
of where the absence stings.
Her note lies face-up beside me.
Stop me, if you can.
And we both know
it isn't a question of can.
I could launch out the window –
a streak of lightning in reverse –
catch her and my unborn boy
on the highway and
lift the car back home,
wheels spinning in the air.
I told her she had
nothing to fear
when she complained
about the blood heavy as grease.
you know Nothing about being human.
When she first held my hand inside hers,
warm as a breath of milk,
she pointed up, asking
what it was like to fly amongst clouds.
Did she imagine
a man cutting through blue sky,
his shadow casting down so low,
nothing but a black mote
proves he's even there?
17JJ
GJ

TAUBA AUERBACH, *SHADOW WEAVE—COMB / COMB I*, 2013
WOVEN CANVAS ON WOODEN STRETCHER, 72" x 54"(182.9 x 137.2 CM)

CONTRIBUTORS

JUDY CHICUREL'S work has appeared in national, regional, and international publications, including *The New York Times*, *Newsday*, and *Granta*. Her plays have been produced and performed in Manhattan. She lives by the water in Brooklyn, New York.

AIMEE BENDER is the award-winning author of five books: *The Girl in the Flammable Skirt* (1998) which was a *NY Times* Notable Book, *An Invisible Sign of My Own* (2000) which was an *LA Times* pick of the year, *Willful Creatures* (2005) which was nominated by *The Believer* as one of the best books of the year, *The Particular Sadness of Lemon Cake* (2010) which recently won the SCIBA award for best fiction, and an Alex Award, and *The Color Master*, released this last August, a *New York Times* Notable book for 2013.

EVAN JAMES'S writing has appeared in the *New York Times*, the *New York Observer*, the *Paris Review Daily*, *The Sun*, and elsewhere. He is a graduate of the Iowa Writers' Workshop, and lives in Brooklyn.

CARL ADAMSHICK'S first book, *Curses and Wishes*, won the Walt Whitman Award from the Academy of American Poets. *Saint Friend*, his second collection of poetry is published with McSweeny's. He founded Tavern Books, a nonprofit publisher dedicated to reviving out-of-print poetry collections. He lives in Portland, Oregon.

ROBIN KIRMAN lives in Tel Aviv and New York. Her novel, *Bradstreet Gate*, will be published by Crown in July 2015.

MONA SIMPSON is the author of *Anywhere but Here*, *My Hollywood*, *A Regular Guy*, *The Lost Father*, *Off Keck Road*, *My Hollywood*, and *Casebook*. Her work has been awarded several prizes: a Whiting Prize, a Guggenheim, a grant from the NEA, a Hodder Fellowship from Princeton University, a Lila Wallace *Readers Digest* Prize, a *Chicago Tribune* Heartland Prize, and most recently a Literature Award from the American Academy of Arts and Letters.

MARTHA RONK is the author of one collection of short fiction, one ironic memoir, and 10 books of poetry, including *Transfer of Qualities*, long listed for the National Book Award in poetry 2013; *Partially Kept'* and *Vertigo*, a National Poetry Series selection 2007. Her forthcoming book is *Optical Proof*.

ALICE BOLIN'S essays are featured in *The Paris Review Daily*, *The New Yorker*'s Page-Turner Blog, *PopMatters*, and *This Recording*. Her poetry has been published in *Guernica*, *Blackbird*, *Washington Square*, and many other journals. She lives in California.

JONATHAN GRIFFIN is a freelance writer based in Los Angeles. He is a contributing editor for *Frieze*, and a regular writer for *Art Review*, *The Art Newspaper*, *Apollo* and *Art Agenda*.

HENRY TAYLOR has had solo exhibitions at MOMA PS1, Santa Monica Museum of Art, and Studio Museum in Harlem. He has also been in group exhibitions, including *Blues for Smoke*, Museum of Contemporary Art, Los Angeles and Whitney Museum of American Art, New York; *Made in LA*, and *30 Americans*, *Henry Taylor*, a new monograph on his work, was published this fall.

DOUGLAS GREENBERG is Distinguished Professor of History at Rutgers University and former Executive Dean of the School of Arts and Sciences there. Previously, he was a Professor of History and Executive Director of the Shoah Foundation Institute at the University of Southern California, President of the Chicago Historical Society, and Vice President of the American Council of Learned Societies. He has also taught history at Rutgers, USC, Princeton, and Lawrence.

DIANA ABU-JABER'S new novel, *Birds Of Paradise*, is the winner of the Arab-American National Book Award. Her novels, *Origin*, *Crescent*, and *Arabian Jazz*, and her memoir *The Language of Baklava*, won several awards, including the PEN Center Award, the American Book Award and the Oregon Book Award. Diana teaches at Portland State University.

SESSHU FOSTER has taught composition and literature in East LA for 20 years, and writing at the University of Iowa, the California Institute for the Arts, the University of California, Santa Cruz and Naropa University's Summer Writing Program. His most recent books are the novel *Atomik Aztex* and *World Ball Notebook*.

RABIH ALAMEDDINE is the author of the novels *Koolaids*, *and I, the Divine*, *The Hakawati*, the story collection, *The Perv*, and most recently, *An Unnecessary Woman*. He divides his time between San Francisco and Beirut.

CARMEN MARIA MACHADO is a fiction writer, critic, and essayist whose work has appeared or is forthcoming in *The New Yorker*, *The Paris Review*, and elsewhere. She was the recipient of the Richard Yates Short Story Prize in 2011, a finalist for the CINTAS Foundation Fellowship in 2013, and a Millay Colony for the Arts fellow in 2014. She is a graduate of the Iowa Writers' Workshop.

DANIEL HANDLER is best known for his work under the pen name Lemony Snicket and his children's books titled *A Series of Unfortunate Events*. The second book in his latest series, *All the Wrong Questions*, is called *When Did You See Her Last?* and was released in October 2013.

JOHN-MANUEL ANDRIOTE has reported on HIV/AIDS as a journalist since 1986, and is the author of *Victory Deferred: How AIDS Changed Gay Life in America*; *Hot Stuff: A Brief History of Disco/Dance Music*, and the forthcoming children's book *Wilhelmina Goes Wandering*, based on the true story of a runaway cow.

LILY TUCK is an American novelist and short story writer, whose novel *The News from Paraguay* won the 2004 National Book Award for Fiction. Her novel *Siam* was nominated for the 2000 PEN/Faulkner Award for Fiction. She has published four other novels, a collection of short stories, and a biography of Italian novelist Elsa Morante.

BENJAMIN ALDES WURGAFT lives in Echo Park, Los Angeles, and currently works at the Massachusetts Institute of Technology where he writes about cultured meat and the futures of food. His scholarly articles, essays, and writings on food culture have appeared in *History and Theory*, *Modern Intellectual History*, *Gastronomica*, *Meatpaper* and other publications, and several books are in the works.

MICHELLE HUNEVEN is a senior fiction editor at the *Los Angeles Review of Books*, and an award-winning novelist. She received an MFA at the Iowa Writers' Workshop. Her novels include *Round Rock*, *Jamesland*, and *Blame*, a finalist for the National Book Critics Circle Award. Her latest is *Off Course*. She teaches creative writing at UCLA.

RAVI MANGLA is the author of the novel *Understudies* (Outpost19, 2013). His work has appeared in *Mid-American Review*, *American Short Fiction*, *The Collagist*, *Gigantic*, *The Rumpus*, *Wigleaf*, and *McSweeney's Internet Tendency*. Follow him on Twitter:@ravi_mangla.

GARY JACKSON is the author of the poetry collection *Missing You, Metropolis*, which received the 2009 Cave Canem Poetry Prize. He is featured on 2013's "New American Poets" by the Poetry Society of America, and his poems have appeared in *Callaloo*, *Tin House*, and elsewhere. He is also the recipient of a Cave Canem and Bread Loaf fellowship. He is a poetry editor at *Catch Up: A Journal of Comics and Literature*, and currently teaches as an Assistant Professor at the College of Charleston.

The MIT Press

SURF CRAFT

Design and the Culture of Board Riding

Richard Kenvin

photographs by Ryan Field

The evolution of the surfboard, from traditional Hawaiian folk designs to masterpieces of mathematical engineering to mass-produced fiberglass.

Copublished with Mingei International Museum, San Diego

THE IMAGINARY APP

edited by Paul D. Miller and Svitlana Matviyenko

The mobile app as technique and imaginary tool, offering a shortcut to instantaneous connection and entertainment.

Software Studies series

TATA DADA

The Real Life and Celestial Adventures of Tristan Tzara

Marius Hentea

The first biography in English of Tristan Tzara, a founder of Dada and one of the most important figures in the European avant-garde.

"… Hentea's attention to poetry compellingly places Tzara in the company of the greatest French poets."
—Andrei Codrescu, author of *The Posthuman Dada Guide: Tzara and Lenin Play Chess*

ALL FOR NOTHING

Hamlet's Negativity

Andrew Cutrofello

"An absorbing study of philosophical thought brought to bear upon the many forms that Hamlet's negativity has taken in critical interpretation."
—David Bevington, University of Chicago, and author of *Murder Most Foul: Hamlet Through the Ages*

Short Circuits series, edited by Slavoj Žižek, Mladen Dolar, and Alenka Zupančič

NO FUTURE FOR YOU

Salvos from *The Baffler*

edited by John Summers, Chris Lehmann and Thomas Frank

"A compendium of literary curveballs"
—*The New York Times*

"Beautifully discontented prose written by people who'd rather be out scrapping. Quite right, too."
—*The Guardian*

COLLISION COURSE

Endless Growth on a Finite Planet

Kerryn Higgs

The story behind the reckless promotion of economic growth despite its disastrous consequences for life on the planet.

392 pp., 6 illus., $29.95 cloth

THE CONSCIOUS MIND

Zoltan Torey

An account of the emergence of the mind: how the brain acquired self-awareness, functional autonomy, the ability to think, and the power of speech.

The MIT Press Essential Knowledge series
208 pp., $13.95 paper

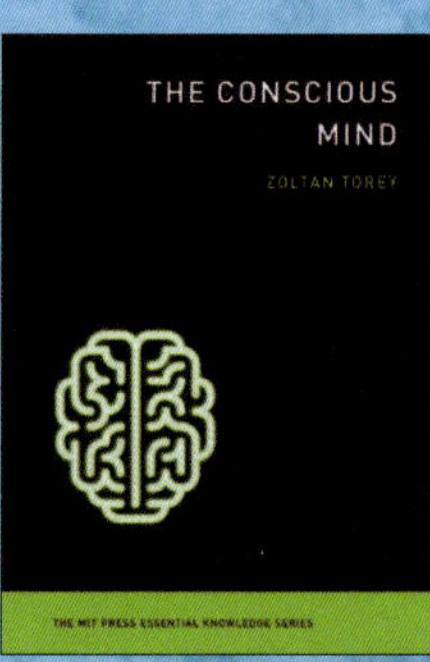

MOOCS

Jonathan Haber

Everything you always wanted to know about MOOCs: an account of massive open online courses and what they might mean for the future of higher education.

The MIT Press Essential Knowledge series

The MIT Press mitpress.mit.edu

DESIRÉE HOLMAN, *MAGNETISM*, 2013
GOUACHE AND PENCIL ON PAPER, 24" x 28"